10 COUNT TRIVIA

EVENTS & CHAMPIONSHIPS

Pocket Books

World
Wrestling
Entertainment®
BOOKS

New York   London   Toronto   Sydney

10 COUNT TRIVIA

EVENTS & CHAMPIONSHIPS

Dean Miller

CONTENTS

INTRODUCTION

How much do you *really* know about pro-
fessional wrestling? Are you an expert on all
things sports entertainment? With this book,
you can finally be absolutely sure, as you can
challenge your friends, impress the ladies,
win bar bets, settle long-standing family
disputes—do it all. The book is filled with
quick ten-question sets, each focused on a
single topic. You don't need to start at the
beginning and work your way through the
book in order. Feel free to jump in and out.
You'll find sets of questions devoted to every
major WWE Pay-Per-View event, including
each of the first twenty-three *WrestleManias*.

In all, there are nearly 1,100 questions
to keep you and your wrestling-obsessed
friends busy for hours—or at least until the
next episode of *Raw*, ECW, or *SmackDown!*
begins.

SECTION I
ROYAL RUMBLE

THE FIRST *ROYAL RUMBLE*

1. Who won the first *Royal Rumble*?
   a. One Man Gang
   b. Jim Duggan
   c. Ultimate Warrior
   d. Junkyard Dog

2. What city played host to the first *Royal Rumble*?
   a. Albany, NY
   b. Richfield, OH
   c. Champaign, IL
   d. Hamilton, Ontario

3. How many entrants were in the first *Royal Rumble* match?
   a. 10   b. 20   c. 30   d. 40

4. Who was the first man eliminated at the first *Royal Rumble* match?
   a. Tito Santana
   b. Jim Neidhart
   c. Boris Zhukov
   d. Harley Race

5. What man lasted the longest at the first *Royal Rumble* match?
   a. Jake Roberts
   b. Bret Hart
   c. Don Muraco
   d. Ron Bass

6. What tag team won WWE Women's Tag Team Championship at the first *Royal Rumble*?
   a. Glamour Girls
   b. Jumping Bomb Angels
   c. Velvet McIntyre & Princess Victoria
   d. Fabulous Moolah & Mae Young

7. What was the result of the Two-Out-of-Three Falls match between the Islanders and the Young Stallions at the first *Royal Rumble*?
   a. Islanders won 2–0.
   c. Islanders won 2–1.
   b. Young Stallions won 2–0.
   d. Young Stallions won 2–1.

8. Who won the opening match at the first *Royal Rumble*?
   a. Rick Rude
   c. Randy Savage
   b. Ricky Steamboat
   d. Roddy Piper

9. Who was the runner-up in the first *Royal Rumble*?
   a. One Man Gang
   c. Ultimate Warrior
   b. Jim Duggan
   d. Junkyard Dog

10. Who signed a contract for a main event match against Hulk Hogan at the first *Royal Rumble*?
   a. Paul Orndorff
   c. King Kong Bundy
   b. Randy Savage
   d. Andre the Giant

ROYAL RUMBLE 1989–1990

1. The first two entrants in *Royal Rumble 1989* were which tag team?
   a. Bushwackers
   c. Strike Force
   b. Demolition
   d. Rockers

2. What Superstar lasted only three seconds in *Royal Rumble 1989*?
   a. Hercules
   b. Warlord
   c. Bushwacker Butch
   d. Bushwacker Luke

3. Hulk Hogan eliminated the most men in *Royal Rumble 1989*. How many?
   a. 7   b. 8   c. 9   d. 10

4. Who won *Royal Rumble 1989*?
   a. Hulk Hogan
   b. Big John Studd
   c. Andre the Giant
   d. Randy Savage

5. What Superstar lasted the longest in *Royal Rumble 1989*?
   a. Mr. Perfect
   b. Greg Valentine
   c. Bad News Brown
   d. Akeem

6. Who set a new record by lasting more than forty-four minutes in *Royal Rumble 1990*?
   a. Ultimate Warrior
   b. Ted DiBiase
   c. Bret Hart
   d. Earthquake

7. In what type of match did Ronnie Garvin and Greg Valentine compete at *Royal Rumble 1990*?
   a. Submission
   b. Street Fight
   c. "I Quit"
   d. Falls Count Anywhere

8. Who was the number thirty entrant and the runner-up at
    Royal Rumble 1990?

    a. Shawn Michaels   c. Mr. Perfect

    b. Rick Rude   d. Barbarian

9. What was the result of the match between Brutus Beefcake
    and the Genius at *Royal Rumble 1990*?

    a. Brutus Beefcake pinned the Genius.

    b. Genius pinned Brutus Beefcake.

    c. Double countout.

    d. Double disqualification.

10. Who defeated Big Boss Man by disqualification at *Royal
    Rumble 1990*?

    a. Jake Roberts   c. Tito Santana

    b. Jim Duggan   d. Bret Hart

ROYAL RUMBLE 1991

1. Who interfered in the Championship match at *Royal
    Rumble 1991*, allowing Sgt. Slaughter to win the WWE
    Championship against the Ultimate Warrior?

    a. Randy Savage   c. Hulk Hogan

    b. Rick Rude   d. Earthquake

2. What new Superstar made his in-ring debut at *Royal
    Rumble 1991*, defeating Koko B. Ware?

    a. Skinner   c. Mountie

    b. Matador   d. Repo Man

3. Who drew the number one position in *Royal Rumble 1991*, making it the second time in the first four *Royal Rumble*s that he'd drawn that entry?
    a. Ted DiBiase
    b. Tito Santana
    c. Bret Hart
    d. Greg Valentine

4. What was the result of the tag match between Ted DiBiase & Virgil vs. Dusty & Dustin Rhodes at *Royal Rumble 1991*?
    a. DiBiase pinned Dusty Rhodes.
    b. Dusty Rhodes pinned DiBiase.
    c. DiBiase pinned Dustin Rhodes.
    d. Dusty Rhodes pinned Virgil.

5. Who was supposed to be entrant number eighteen in *Royal Rumble 1991* but never entered?
    a. Rick Rude
    b. Dino Bravo
    c. Randy Savage
    d. Jake Roberts

6. Who lasted more than fifty-two minutes in *Royal Rumble 1991*, setting a new record?
    a. Hercules
    b. Bret Hart
    c. Greg Valentine
    d. Rick Martel

7. The Rockers defeated what tag team in the opening match of *Royal Rumble 1991*?
    a. Demolition
    b. Rhythm & Blues
    c. Orient Express
    d. Nasty Boys

8. Who won *Royal Rumble 1991*?
   a. Hulk Hogan
   b. Ric Flair
   c. Davey Boy Smith
   d. Randy Savage

9. Who was the runner-up of *Royal Rumble 1991*?
   a. Barbarian
   b. Mr. Perfect
   c. Earthquake
   d. Undertaker

10. What member of the Heenan family did Big Boss Man defeat in a singles match at *Royal Rumble 1991*?
    a. Mr. Perfect
    b. Barbarian
    c. Rick Rude
    d. Hercules

ROYAL RUMBLE 1992–1993

1. Who was the first man eliminated from *Royal Rumble 1992*?
   a. Shawn Michaels
   b. Ted DiBiase
   c. Texas Tornado
   d. Big Boss Man

2. Ric Flair set a new longevity record at *Royal Rumble 1992*. What was his entry number?
   a. 1   b. 2   c. 3   d. 5

3. Who lasted more than thirty minutes in *Royal Rumble 1992*, despite having wrestled for the Intercontinental Championship earlier that evening?
   a. Bret Hart
   b. Shawn Michaels
   c. Mr. Perfect
   d. Roddy Piper

4. Who was in the Bushwackers' corner for their match against the Beverly Brothers at *Royal Rumble 1992*?
   a. Gobbledy Gooker
   b. Jamison
   c. Bertha Faye
   d. Gillberg

5. Who helped Ric Flair eliminate Sid Justice, making Flair the WWE Champion at *Royal Rumble 1992*?
   a. Mr. Perfect
   b. Jake Roberts
   c. Hulk Hogan
   d. Randy Savage

6. Who competed in his sixth consecutive *Royal Rumble* in 1993, making him the only Superstar to enter each of the first six *Royal Rumble* matches?
   a. Jake Roberts
   b. Rick Martel
   c. Tito Santana
   d. Koko B. Ware

7. What Superstar eliminated Undertaker from *Royal Rumble 1993*, despite not being a participant in the match?
   a. Kama
   b. King Kong Bundy
   c. Giant Gonzales
   d. Diesel

8. In *Royal Rumble 1993*, who became the first Superstar to last more than one hour in a *Royal Rumble* match?
   a. Ric Flair
   b. Ted DiBiase
   c. Jerry Lawler
   d. Bob Backlund

9. Who won *Royal Rumble 1993*?
   a. Yokozuna
   b. Randy Savage
   c. Lex Luger
   d. Mr. Perfect

10. Who challenged Bret Hart for the Championship at *Royal Rumble 1993*?

    a. Diesel   c. Razor Ramon

    b. Bam Bam Bigelow d. Shawn Michaels

ROYAL RUMBLE 1994–1995

1. Who challenged Razor Ramon for the Intercontinental Championship at *Royal Rumble 1994*?

    a. Shawn Michaels   c. Irwin R. Shyster

    b. 1-2-3 Kid   d. Tatanka

2. What was the result of the Casket match between Yokozuna and Undertaker at *Royal Rumble 1994*?

    a. Undertaker locked Yokozuna in the casket.

    b. Yokozuna locked Undertaker in the casket.

    c. Undertaker won by countout when Yokozuna ran away.

    d. Undertaker locked Mr. Fuji and Jim Cornette in the casket.

3. How many consecutive Superstars did Diesel eliminate in *Royal Rumble 1994*?

    a. 6   b. 7   c. 8   d. 9

4. Who lasted the longest in *Royal Rumble 1994*?

    a. Shawn Michaels   c. Bam Bam Bigelow

    b. Crush   d. Greg Valentine

5. How did the Quebecers retain their WWE World Tag Team Championship against Bret Hart & Owen Hart at *Royal Rumble 1994?*
    a. Quebecers pinned Owen.
    b. Quebecers pinned Bret.
    c. The referee stopped the match due to injury to Bret.
    d. Harts were disqualified.

6. What was the result of the WWE Championship match between Diesel and Bret Hart at *Royal Rumble 1995?*
    a. Diesel pinned Hart.
    b. Hart pinned Diesel.
    c. Diesel was disqualified.
    d. The match was declared a draw.

7. Who won the Intercontinental Championship at *Royal Rumble 1995?*
    a. Jeff Jarrett   c. Rick Martel
    b. Razor Ramon   d. Ted DiBiase

8. What team won the vacant Tag Team Championship at *Royal Rumble 1995?*
    a. Smokin' Gunns
    b. Tatanka & Bam Bam Bigelow
    c. Owen Hart & Yokozuna
    d. Bob Holly & the 1-2-3 Kid

9. Which Superstar did *not* interfere in the WWE Championship match between Bret Hart and Diesel at *Royal Rumble 1995*?
   a. Bob Backlund
   b. Razor Ramon
   c. Shawn Michaels
   d. Jeff Jarrett

10. Who became the first Superstar to win the *Rumble* from the number one entry position at *Royal Rumble 1995*?
    a. Davey Boy Smith
    b. Shawn Michaels
    c. Lex Luger
    d. Bob Backlund

ROYAL RUMBLE 1996–1997

1. Who interfered in the Championship match between Undertaker and Bret Hart at *Royal Rumble 1996*?
   a. Shawn Michaels
   b. Triple H
   c. Diesel
   d. Sycho Sid

2. Triple H lasted the longest in *Royal Rumble 1996*, more than forty-eight minutes. How many Superstars did he eliminate?
   a. 0   b. 1   c. 3   d. 5

3. Who won the pre–*Royal Rumble* Free-For-All for the right to enter *Royal Rumble 1996* as number thirty?
   a. Tatanka
   b. Duke Droese
   c. British Bulldog
   d. Kama

4. Who illegally reentered the ring and eliminated three Superstars from *Royal Rumble 1996* after he was eliminated?
   a. King Mabel
   b. Vader
   c. Owen Hart
   d. Yokozuna

5. Who won the Intercontinental Championship at *Royal Rumble 1996*?
   a. Razor Ramon
   b. Jeff Jarrett
   c. Goldust
   d. 1-2-3 Kid

6. Who left *Royal Rumble 1996* as the WWE World Tag Team Champions?
   a. Bodydonnas
   b. Godwinns
   c. Smokin' Gunns
   d. Owen Hart & Yokozuna

7. Who won the WWE Championship at *Royal Rumble 1997*?
   a. Sycho Sid
   b. Undertaker
   c. Shawn Michaels
   d. Vader

8. Who challenged Triple H for the Intercontinental Championship at *Royal Rumble 1997*?
   a. The Rock
   b. Ahmed Johnson
   c. Goldust
   d. Owen Hart

9. Stone Cold Steve Austin reentered *Royal Rumble 1997* after being eliminated and went on to win the match. Who had eliminated Stone Cold?
   a. Vader
   b. Undertaker
   c. Diesel
   d. Bret Hart

10. How many Superstars did Steve Austin eliminate from
    Royal Rumble 1997?

    a. 8   b. 9   c. 10   d. 11

ROYAL RUMBLE 1998–1999

1. All three of Mick Foley's personalities (Mankind, Cactus
   Jack, and Dude Love) entered *Royal Rumble 1998*. Who did
   not eliminate one of Mick Foley's personalities?

   a. Chainsaw Charlie   c. The Rock
   b. Goldust   d. Faarooq

2. Even though Triple H and Chyna were not participants in
   Royal Rumble 1998, they did eliminate a Superstar. Whom
   did they eliminate?

   a. Marc Mero   c. Vader
   b. Jeff Jarrett   d. Owen Hart

3. In what type of match did Shawn Michaels and
   Undertaker compete for the WWE Championship at *Royal
   Rumble 1998*?

   a. Hell in a Cell   c. Buried Alive
   b. Ladder   d. Casket

4. Who was the special guest referee when Max Mini, Mosiac,
   and Nova faced Battalion, El Torito, and Tarantula at *Royal
   Rumble 1998*?

   a. Luna Vachon   c. Sunny
   b. Sable   d. Debra

5. Whom did Stone Cold Steve Austin eliminate last to win *Royal Rumble 1998*?
   a. Faarooq
   b. The Rock
   c. Ken Shamrock
   d. Bradshaw

6. When Mr. McMahon won *Royal Rumble 1999*, how many Superstars did he eliminate?
   a. 0   b. 1   c. 2   d. 4

7. Who won a Corporate *Royal Rumble* to win the number thirty entry in *Royal Rumble 1999*?
   a. Big Boss Man
   b. Chyna
   c. X-Pac
   d. Ken Shamrock

8. In what type of match did Sable and Luna Vachon compete for the Women's Championship at *Royal Rumble 1999*?
   a. Evening Gown
   b. Two-Out-of-Three Falls
   c. Strap
   d. Hardcore

9. Whom did The Rock defeat in an "I Quit" match at *Royal Rumble 1999* to win the WWE Championship?
   a. Undertaker
   b. Kane
   c. Triple H
   d. Mankind

10. Who left *Royal Rumble 1999* as the Intercontinental Champion?
    a. Ken Shamrock
    b. Billy Gunn
    c. Val Venis
    d. Christian

ROYAL RUMBLE 2000–2001

1. Chris Jericho and Chyna were coholders of the Intercontinental Championship going into their Triple-Threat match for the title at *Royal Rumble 2000*. Who was the third participant in the match?
   a. D'Lo Brown
   b. Test
   c. Hardcore Holly
   d. Al Snow

2. Who eliminated the first seven Superstars from *Royal Rumble 2000*?
   a. Big Show
   b. Rikishi
   c. Kane
   d. British Bulldog

3. What team challenged the New Age Outlaws for the WWE World Tag Team Championship at *Royal Rumble 2000*?
   a. Edge & Christian
   b. Headbangers
   c. Acolytes
   d. Hardy Boys

4. In what type of match did Triple H and Cactus Jack wrestle at *Royal Rumble 2000*?
   a. Sledgehammer on a Pole
   b. Falls Count Anywhere
   c. Street Fight
   d. Last Man Standing

5. Who won the Miss Rumble 2000 Swimsuit Competition at *Royal Rumble 2000*?
   a. Kat
   b. Mae Young
   c. Luna
   d. Terri

6. Who accompanied Ivory to the ring for her WWE
   Women's Championship match at *Royal Rumble 2001*?
   a. Val Venis   c. Godfather
   b. Steven Richards   d. Crash Holly

7. How many Superstars did Kane eliminate from *Royal
   Rumble 2001*?
   a. 9   b. 10   c. 11   d. 12

8. Who accompanied Kurt Angle to the ring for his
   Championship match against Triple H at *Royal Rumble
   2001*?
   a. Stephanie McMahon   c. Trish Stratus
   b. Stacy Keibler   d. Terri

9. The winner of *Royal Rumble 2001* became a three-time
   Royal Rumble winner. Through 2001, which of the
   following Superstars had *not* won multiple *Royal Rumbles*?
   a. Steve Austin   c. Hulk Hogan
   b. The Rock   d. Shawn Michaels

10. Who won the Intercontinental Championship in a Ladder
    match at *Royal Rumble 2001*?
    a. Jeff Hardy   c. Chris Jericho
    b. Edge   d. Christian

ROYAL RUMBLE 2002–2003

1. Who shockingly eliminated Undertaker from *Royal Rumble 2002*?
   a. Hurricane
   b. Maven
   c. Jamie Noble
   d. Scotty 2 Hotty

2. Who was the runner-up to Triple H in *Royal Rumble 2002*?
   a. Kane
   b. Kurt Angle
   c. Big Show
   d. Mr. Perfect

3. Who challenged Chris Jericho for the Undisputed Championship at *Royal Rumble 2002*?
   a. Booker T
   b. Steve Austin
   c. The Rock
   d. Big Show

4. What was the result of the Street Fight between Mr. McMahon and Ric Flair at *Royal Rumble 2002*?
   a. Mr. McMahon pinned Flair.
   b. Flair made Mr. McMahon submit.
   c. Flair won by disqualification.
   d. Mr. McMahon won by disqualification.

5. Who was the special guest referee when Trish Stratus and Jazz met for the WWE Women's Championship at *Royal Rumble 2002*?
   a. Val Venis
   b. Jacqueline
   c. Lita
   d. Victoria

6. Who had to win a qualifying match at the beginning of *Royal Rumble 2003* in order to enter the match?
   a. Batista
   b. Undertaker
   c. Big Show
   d. Brock Lesnar

7. What was the result of the World Heavyweight Championship match between Triple H and Scott Steiner at *Royal Rumble 2003*?
   a. Scott Steiner won by disqualification.
   b. Triple H won by disqualification.
   c. The match was declared no contest.
   d. Both men were counted out.

8. Who drew entry number one and was the first man eliminated from *Royal Rumble 2003*?
   a. Chris Jericho
   b. Rey Mysterio
   c. Edge
   d. Shawn Michaels

9. Who was the runner-up in *Royal Rumble 2003*?
   a. Batista
   b. Kane
   c. Undertaker
   d. Rob Van Dam

10. What duo successfully defended the World Tag Team Championship at *Royal Rumble 2003*?
    a. Dudley Boys
    b. William Regal & Lance Storm
    c. Booker T & Goldust
    d. 3 Minute Warning

ROYAL RUMBLE 2004–2005

1. What Superstar drew the number thirteen entry in *Royal Rumble 2004* but never entered because he was attacked by Kane before reaching the ring?
   a. A-Train
   b. Rico
   c. Spike Dudley
   d. Nunzio

2. Who challenged Brock Lesnar for the WWE Championship at *Royal Rumble 2004*?
   a. Kurt Angle
   b. Eddie Guerrero
   c. Hardcore Holly
   d. Christian

3. Who was a late entry in *Royal Rumble 2004* and eliminated only Randy Orton and himself?
   a. John Cena
   b. Ric Flair
   c. Mick Foley
   d. Kurt Angle

4. What was the result of the Last Man Standing match for the World Heavyweight Championship between Triple H and Shawn Michaels at *Royal Rumble 2004*?
   a. Triple H won.
   b. Shawn Michaels won.
   c. A double countout.
   d. No contest.

5. What tag team successfully defended the World Tag Team Championship at *Royal Rumble 2004?*
   a. Dudley Boys
   b. Evolution
   c. World's Greatest Tag Team
   d. Chris Jericho & Christian

6. Who was attacked on his way to the ring by an eliminated Muhammad Hassan and was unable to enter *Royal Rumble 2005?*
   a. Simon Dean   c. Paul London
   b. Scotty 2 Hotty   d. Charlie Haas

7. Kurt Angle entered *Royal Rumble 2005* by stealing the number of what participant backstage?
   a. Orlando Jordan   c. Nunzio
   b. Jonathan Coachman   d. Daniel Puder

8. Whom did Batista last eliminate when he won *Royal Rumble 2005?*
   a. Kane   c. Edge
   b. Ric Flair   d. John Cena

9. In what type of match did JBL defend the WWE Championship at *Royal Rumble 2005?*
   a. Fatal Four Way   c. Street Fight
   b. Triple-Threat   d. Falls Count Anywhere

10. Whom did Undertaker face in a Casket match at *Royal Rumble 2005*?
   - a. Snitsky
   - b. Heidenreich
   - c. Big Show
   - d. Booker T

ROYAL RUMBLE 2006–2007

1. Who won the Six-Way Cruiserweight match to win the Cruiserweight Championship at *Royal Rumble 2006*?
   - a. Paul London
   - b. Gregory Helms
   - c. Jamie Noble
   - d. Nunzio

2. Who set a new record for longevity in the ring on his way to winning *Royal Rumble 2006*?
   - a. Rey Mysterio
   - b. Randy Orton
   - c. Triple H
   - d. Ric Flair

3. Who eliminated Shawn Michaels from *Royal Rumble 2006* despite not being in the match?
   - a. JBL
   - b. Mr. McMahon
   - c. Shane McMahon
   - d. Triple H

4. Who was the special guest referee for the Mickie James vs. Ashley match at *Royal Rumble 2006*?
   - a. Lita
   - b. Trish Stratus
   - c. Melina
   - d. Victoria

5. Who challenged Kurt Angle for the World Heavyweight Championship at *Royal Rumble 2006*?
   a. Undertaker
   b. Mark Henry
   c. Edge
   d. Finlay

6. Undertaker won *Royal Rumble 2007* after entering from what position?
   a. #15   b. #20   c. #25   d. #30

7. Who returned to the ring after being eliminated from *Royal Rumble 2007* and eliminated Kane?
   a. Great Khali
   b. King Booker
   c. Sabu
   d. Randy Orton

8. What was the result of the ECW Championship match between Bobby Lashley and Test at *Royal Rumble 2007*?
   a. Lashley pinned Test.
   b. Lashley won by disqualification.
   c. Test won by disqualification.
   d. Lashley won by countout.

9. In what type of match did John Cena and Umaga compete for the WWE Championship at *Royal Rumble 2007*?
   a. Steel Cage
   b. Falls Count Anywhere
   c. TLC
   d. Last Man Standing

10. What ECW representative lasted the longest in *Royal Rumble 2007*?
    a. Rob Van Dam
    b. CM Punk
    c. Tommy Dreamer
    d. Sandman

SECTION II
GOLD RUSH

INTERCONTINENTAL CHAMPIONSHIP

1. Who was the first Intercontinental Champion?
   - a. Ken Patera
   - b. Ted DiBiase
   - c. Don Muraco
   - d. Pat Patterson

2. Who became the first seven-time Intercontinental Champion at *Unforgiven 2004*?
   - a. Edge
   - b. Rob Van Dam
   - c. Chris Jericho
   - d. Christian

3. In what country did Santino Marella win the Intercontinental Championship in his debut match in 2007?
   - a. England
   - b. Germany
   - c. Spain
   - d. Italy

4. Who was the first Superstar to win the Intercontinental Championship at a *WrestleMania*?
   - a. Randy Savage
   - b. Honky Tonk Man
   - c. Ricky Steamboat
   - d. Rick Rude

5. Who won the tournament to crown a new Intercontinental Champion after *WrestleMania VI*?
   - a. Tito Santana
   - b. Rick Rude
   - c. Mr. Perfect
   - d. Texas Tornado

6. Whom did Stone Cold Steve Austin defeat to win his first Intercontinental Championship at *SummerSlam 1997*?
   a. Owen Hart
   b. Rock
   c. Triple H
   d. Marc Mero

7. In October 1995, who was awarded the Intercontinental Championship at *In Your House*, only to lose it the same night?
   a. Goldust
   b. Razor Ramon
   c. Owen Hart
   d. Dean Douglas

8. Who was the first Superstar to hold the Intercontinental Championship for more than one year?
   a. Ken Patera
   b. Honky Tonk Man
   c. Pedro Morales
   d. Tito Santana

9. As a result of a double pinfall, what two Superstars were considered Intercontinental Cochampions from January 3 to 23, 2000?
   a. Jeff Jarrett and Owen Hart
   b. Chris Jericho and Kurt Angle
   c. Jeff Jarrett and Chyna
   d. Chris Jericho and Chyna

10. Who won a battle royal to become the Intercontinental Champion at *Judgment Day 2003* after the title had been inactive for more than half a year?
    a. Chris Jericho
    b. Christian
    c. Booker T
    d. Rob Van Dam

EUROPEAN CHAMPIONSHIP

1. Who was the first European champion?
    a. Owen Hart
    b. British Bulldog
    c. Roddy Piper
    d. Shawn Michaels

2. Who was the first Superstar to hold the European Championship and Intercontinental Championship at the same time?
    a. D'Lo Brown
    b. Triple H
    c. X-Pac
    d. Jeff Jarrett

3. In what country was the initial tournament held to award the European Championship?
    a. England
    b. Canada
    c. Italy
    d. Germany

4. Who temporarily deactivated the European Championship, attempting to retire as European Champion?
    a. Shawn Michaels
    b. Kurt Angle
    c. D'Lo Brown
    d. Shane McMahon

5. What was the first *WrestleMania* that featured a title defense of the European Championship?
    a. *WrestleMania XII*
    b. *WrestleMania 13*
    c. *WrestleMania XIV*
    d. *WrestleMania XV*

6. Who is the only Superstar, other than D'Lo Brown, to hold the European Championship on four separate occasions?
   a. Edge
   b. Eddie Guerrero
   c. Val Venis
   d. William Regal

7. Who unified the European and Intercontinental championships in July 2002, retiring the European Championship?
   a. Jeff Hardy
   b. Rob Van Dam
   c. Spike Dudley
   d. Hurricane

8. Who was the first two-time European Champion?
   a. British Bulldog
   b. X-Pac
   c. D'Lo Brown
   d. Triple H

9. Who was the first Superstar to win the European championship at a *WrestleMania*?
   a. Mark Henry
   b. Al Snow
   c. British Bulldog
   d. Chris Jericho

10. After the British Bulldog, who had the second longest European Championship reign?
    a. X-Pac
    b. Triple H
    c. Matt Hardy
    d. Christian

WWE CRUISERWEIGHT CHAMPIONSHIP

1. Who was the last Superstar to win the WWE Cruiserweight Championship on an episode of *Raw*?
   - a. Spike Dudley
   - b. Billy Kidman
   - c. Tajiri
   - d. Hurricane

2. Only four Superstars held the WWE Cruiserweight Championship in 2003. Which Superstar held it the longest that year?
   - a. Rey Mysterio
   - b. Matt Hardy
   - c. Billy Kidman
   - d. Tajiri

3. In May 2004, Chavo Guerrero was Cruiserweight Champion for only two days. Who ended his reign?
   - a. Jacqueline
   - b. Paul London
   - c. Chavo Classic
   - d. Rey Mysterio

4. Who stripped Hornswoggle of the Cruiserweight Championship in August 2007?
   - a. Teddy Long
   - b. Mr. McMahon
   - c. Finlay
   - d. Vickie Guerrero

5. In November 2005, who won the Cruiserweight Championship in Rome, Italy?
   - a. Nunzio
   - b. Kid Kash
   - c. Juventud
   - d. Funaki

6. Whom did Hornswoggle pin during the Cruiserweight Open at *Great American Bash 2007* to win the championship?

    a. Scotty 2 Hotty
    b. Jamie Noble
    c. Shannon Moore
    d. Jimmy Wang Yang

7. Who jumped from the *Raw* roster to win the Cruiserweight Championship at *Royal Rumble 2007*?

    a. Daivari
    b. Gregory Helms
    c. Super Crazy
    d. Paul London

8. Of Rey Mysterio's eight reigns as Cruiserweight Champion in WCW and WWE, how many of those have occurred in WWE?

    a. 2　　　b. 3　　　c. 4　　　d. 5

9. Who was Cruiserweight Champion in May 2002 when the World Wrestling Federation became World Wrestling Entertainment?

    a. Billy Kidman
    b. Hurricane
    c. Tajiri
    d. X-Pac

10. Paul London became Cruiserweight Champion in March 2005 by winning a battle royal featuring how many Superstars?

    a. 4　　　b. 6　　　c. 8　　　d. 10

HARDCORE CHAMPIONSHIP

1. What Superstar introduced the 24/7 Rule for the WWE Hardcore Championship by proclaiming he would defend the championship at any and all times?
   a. Al Snow
   b. Crash Holly
   c. Hardcore Holly
   d. Tazz

2. Which Diva never held the WWE Hardcore Championship?
   a. Molly Holly
   b. Trish Stratus
   c. Terri Runnels
   d. Lita

3. Who briefly renamed the WWE Hardcore Championship the Texas Hardcore Championship?
   a. Bradshaw
   b. Steve Austin
   c. Terry Funk
   d. Shawn Michaels

4. Who held the WWE Hardcore Championship an amazing twenty-seven times?
   a. Crash Holly
   b. Mankind
   c. Tazz
   d. Raven

5. The original WWE Hardcore Championship belt was a smashed version of the WWE Championship belt from the time that Hulk Hogan was champion. Who destroyed the belt?
   a. Earthquake
   b. Jake Roberts
   c. Mr. Perfect
   d. Sgt. Slaughter

6. What WWE Hardcore Champion did Rob Van Dam defeat to unify the Championship with the Intercontinental Championship in August 2002?

   a. Steven Richards
   b. Tommy Dreamer
   c. Shawn Stasiak
   d. Bradshaw

7. Whom did Undertaker defeat for his only WWE Hardcore Championship title?

   a. Raven
   b. Rob Van Dam
   c. Maven
   d. Jeff Hardy

8. Who was the first three-time WWE Hardcore Champion?

   a. Al Snow
   b. Hardcore Holly
   c. Billy Gunn
   d. Big Boss Man

9. Who, at ninety-seven days, had the longest WWE Hardcore Championship reign?

   a. Al Snow
   b. Hardcore Holly
   c. Billy Gunn
   d. Big Boss Man

10. Who was the first Superstar to win the WWE Hardcore Championship under the 24/7 Rule?

    a. Viscera
    b. Funaki
    c. Pete Gas
    d. Perry Saturn

WWE CHAMPIONSHIP

1. Which Superstar never won the WWE Championship in a sixty-minute Iron Man match?
    a. Shawn Michaels
    b. Triple H
    c. Kurt Angle
    d. Brock Lesnar

2. What man ended Bruno Sammartino's historic eight-year reign as WWE Champion in January 1971?
    a. Stan Stasiak
    b. Pedro Morales
    c. Buddy Rogers
    d. Ivan Koloff

3. Who was the first man to win the WWE Championship at the *Royal Rumble?*
    a. Ric Flair
    b. Sgt. Slaughter
    c. Randy Savage
    d. Bret Hart

4. Who was the first man to win and lose the WWE Championship on the same day?
    a. Andre the Giant
    b. Yokozuna
    c. Bob Backlund
    d. Superstar Billy Graham

5. At what Pay-Per-View event did Undertaker win his first WWE Championship?
    a. *Royal Rumble*
    b. *WrestleMania*
    c. *SummerSlam*
    d. *Survivor Series*

6. Who was the first man to win the WWE Championship in a Ladder match?
   a. The Rock
   b. Shawn Michaels
   c. Edge
   d. Triple H

7. How many times did the WWE Championship change hands in 2005?
   a. 1   b. 3   c. 5   d. 7

8. Who was WWE Champion, in September 2002, when the title became exclusive to *SmackDown!*?
   a. Kurt Angle
   b. The Rock
   c. Brock Lesnar
   d. Undertaker

9. At what Pay-Per-View event did Edge cash in his *WrestleMania 21* Money in the Bank title shot and become WWE Champion?
   a. *No Way Out*
   b. *One Night Stand*
   c. *Armageddon*
   d. *New Year's Revolution*

10. Which Superstar never defeated Bret Hart for the WWE Championship?
    a. Yokozuna
    b. Bob Backlund
    c. Diesel
    d. Sycho Sid

WWE WOMEN'S CHAMPIONSHIP

1. When WWE brought back the Women's Championship in 1993, who won the tournament to decide the champion?
    a. Heidi Lee Morgan
    c. Bull Nakano
    b. Alundra Blayze
    d. Bertha Faye

2. Who was revealed to be the Spider Lady after she beat Wendi Richter for the WWE Women's Championship in 1985?
    a. Sensational Sherri
    c. Bertha Faye
    b. Mae Young
    d. Fabulous Moolah

3. Whom did Stephanie McMahon defeat for her first and only WWE Women's Championship reign?
    a. Miss Kitty
    c. Lita
    b. Ivory
    d. Jacqueline

4. What WWE Diva won the Women's Championship in her debut match in 2003, a Seven-Woman Battle Royal?
    a. Victoria
    c. Gail Kim
    b. Molly Holly
    d. Tori

5. When Trish Stratus won the WWE Women's Championship at *Unforgiven 2006*, it marked what number championship reign for her?
    a. 5
    b. 6
    c. 7
    d. 8

6. In what type of match did Deborah defeat Sable to win the WWE Women's Championship in May 1999?
   - a. Bra and Panties
   - b. Lumberjill
   - c. Fatal Four Way
   - d. Evening Gown

7. Whom did Melina defeat for her first WWE Women's Championship in February 2007?
   - a. Candice Michelle
   - b. Victoria
   - c. Torrie Wilson
   - d. Mickie James

8. At what 2007 PPV did Beth Phoenix win her first WWE Women's Championship?
   - a. *Backlash*
   - b. *SummerSlam*
   - c. *Unforgiven*
   - d. *Great American Bash*

9. What male former WWE manager won the WWE Women's Championship disguised as a woman?
   - a. Jimmy Hart
   - b. Brother Love
   - c. Harvey Wippleman
   - d. Clarence Mason

10. What Diva won the WWE Women's Championship in a Six-Way match at *Survivor Series 2001*?
    - a. Jazz
    - b. Ivory
    - c. Molly Holly
    - d. Trish Stratus

SECTION III
NO WAY OUT

NO WAY OUT 1998–2001

1. What future WWE Champion challenged Jeff Jarrett for
    the NWA North American Heavyweight Championship at
    No Way Out 1998?
    a. Eddie Guerrero   c. Triple H
    b. Bradshaw   d. Edge

2. Who successfully defended the WWE Light Heavyweight
    Championship at *No Way Out 1998*?
    a. Scotty 2 Hotty   c. Dean Malenko
    b. Pantera   d. Taka Michinoku

3. Who got the pin when Ken Shamrock, Ahmed Johnson,
    and Disciples of Apocalypse defeated Nation of
    Domination at *No Way Out 1998*?
    a. Ken Shamrock   c. Skull
    b. Ahmed Johnson   d. 8 Ball

4. Shawn Michaels was supposed to be on the team that
    challenged Steve Austin, Owen Hart, Cactus Jack, and
    Chainsaw Charlie at *No Way Out 1998*, but he had to be
    replaced due to injury. Who took his place?
    a. Vader   c. Savio Vega
    b. Jacques Rougeau   d. Kane

5. Who won the Intercontinental Championship at *No Way Out 2000*?

   a. Chyna

   b. Chris Jericho

   c. Kurt Angle

   d. Rikishi

6. In what type of match did X-Pac and Kane participate at *No Way Out 2000*?

   a. Ladder

   b. Street Fight

   c. No Holds Barred

   d. Inferno

7. Who interfered in the match at *No Way Out 2000*, allowing Edge & Christian to defeat the Hardy Boys?

   a. Gangrel

   b. Terri Runnels

   c. Michael Hayes

   d. Kurt Angle

8. What Superstar helped Stephanie McMahon-Helmsley defeat Trish Stratus at *No Way Out 2001*?

   a. Kurt Angle

   b. Triple H

   c. William Regal

   d. Mark Henry

9. Who was forced to join the Right to Censor as a result of Steven Richards's victory over Jerry Lawler at *No Way Out 2001*?

   a. Jim Ross

   b. Ivory

   c. Kat

   d. Jerry Lawler

10. Who won the WWE Championship at *No Way Out 2001*?

   a. The Rock

   b. Kurt Angle

   c. Big Show

   d. Triple H

NO WAY OUT 2002–2004

1. Who won the Tag Team Turmoil match at *No Way Out* 2002 to earn a WWE World Tag Team Championship Opportunity at *WrestleMania X8*?
   a. Hardy Boys
   b. APA
   c. Dudley Boys
   d. Billy & Chuck

2. In what type of match did William Regal and Edge compete for the Intercontinental Championship at *No Way Out 2002*?
   a. Brass Knuckles on a Pole
   b. Hair
   c. Two-Out-of-Three Falls
   d. Submission

3. Whom did the nWo attack at the conclusion of *No Way Out 2002*?
   a. The Rock
   b. Steve Austin
   c. Triple H
   d. Undertaker

4. Who won the WWE Cruiserweight Championship at *No Way Out 2003*?
   a. Billy Kidman
   b. Matt Hardy
   c. Scotty 2 Hotty
   d. Jamie Noble

5. Who faced Eric Bischoff at *No Way Out 2003*?
   a. Shane McMahon
   b. Chris Jericho
   c. Steve Austin
   d. Paul Heyman

6. Who successfully defended the WWE World Tag Team Championship at *No Way Out 2003*?
   a. Kane & Rob Van Dam
   b. William Regal & Lance Storm
   c. Booker T & Goldust
   d. Test & Scott Steiner

7. In what type of match did Jamie Noble & Nidia compete at *No Way Out 2004*?
   a. Tuxedo vs. Evening Gown   c. Chain
   b. Blindfold   d. Arm Wrestling

8. Who did Kurt Angle force to submit at *No Way Out 2004* in order to win a WWE Championship shot at *WrestleMania XX*?
   a. Big Show   c. Hardcore Holly
   b. John Cena   d. Edge

9. Who got the pin when Rikishi & Scotty 2 Hotty faced the Basham Brothers & Shaniqua in a Mixed Handicap match at *No Way Out 2004*?
   a. Shaniqua   c. Scotty 2 Hotty
   b. Rikishi   d. Danny Basham

10. Who was in Rey Mysterio's corner for his match against Chavo Guerrero at *No Way Out 2004*?
    a. Oscar De La Hoya   c. Felix Trinidad
    b. Jorge Paez   d. Julio Caesar Chavez

NO WAY OUT 2005–2007

1. Chavo Guerrero won the Cruiserweight Open at *No Way Out 2005*. Whom did he last eliminate to win the match?
   a. Spike Dudley
   b. Paul London
   c. Shannon Moore
   d. Funaki

2. Whom did John Cena defeat to become the number one contender to the WWE Championship at *No Way Out 2005?*
   a. Eddie Guerrero
   b. Booker T
   c. Kurt Angle
   d. Undertaker

3. Who left *No Way Out 2006* as the WWE Cruiserweight Champion?
   a. Scotty 2 Hotty
   b. Kid Kash
   c. Psicosis
   d. Gregory Helms

4. Who helped JBL defeat Bobby Lashley at *No Way Out 2006?*
   a. Great Khali
   b. Finlay
   c. William Regal
   d. Mr. Kennedy

5. Who teamed with Matt Hardy to defeat MNM at *No Way Out 2006?*
   a. Jim Duggan
   b. Boogeyman
   c. Tatanka
   d. Brian Kendrick

6. Who defeated Rey Mysterio for his *WrestleMania 22* World
   Title Opportunity at *No Way Out 2006*?
   a. Booker T   c. Randy Orton
   b. Undertaker   d. Batista

7. What WWE Diva won the Talent Invitational at *No Way
   Out 2007*?
   a. Ariel   c. Kelly Kelly
   b. Ashley   d. Jillian Hall

8. Who recorded the pin when John Cena & Shawn Michaels
   met Batista & Undertaker at *No Way Out 2007*?
   a. John Cena   c. Batista
   b. Shawn Michaels   d. Undertaker

9. Who won the Cruiserweight Open for the WWE
   Cruiserweight Championship at *No Way Out 2007*?
   a. Jimmy Yang Wang   c. Chavo Guerrero
   b. Gregory Helms   d. Funaki

10. Who recorded the pin when Finlay & Hornswoggle met
    Boogeyman & Little Boogeyman at *No Way Out 2007*?
    a. Finlay   c. Boogeyman
    b. Hornswoggle   d. Little Boogeyman

SECTION IV
WRESTLEMANIA

WRESTLEMANIA

1. What city was host to the first *WrestleMania*?
   a. Philadelphia
   c. New York
   b. Washington, D.C.
   d. Boston

2. Who was in the corner of Hulk Hogan and Mr. T for the main event?
   a. Jake Roberts
   c. Jimmy Snuka
   b. Tito Santana
   d. Rocky Johnson

3. Who managed Nikolai Volkoff & Iron Sheik when they won the WWE Tag Team Championship at *WrestleMania*?
   a. Jimmy Hart
   c. Johnny Valiant
   b. Capt. Lou Albano
   d. "Classy" Freddie Blassie

4. Who won the opening match of the first *WrestleMania*?
   a. Junkyard Dog
   c. King Kong Bundy
   b. Tito Santana
   d. Brutus Beefcake

5. What boxing legend served as guest referee for the main event of *WrestleMania*?
   a. George Foreman
   c. Sugar Ray Leonard
   b. Joe Frazier
   d. Muhammad Ali

6. The team of Hulk Hogan and Mr. T were victorious in the first *WrestleMania*'s main event. How did they obtain their victory?
   a. Hulk Hogan pinned Roddy Piper.
   b. Hulk Hogan pinned Paul Orndorff.
   c. Mr. T pinned Roddy Piper.
   d. Mr. T pinned Paul Orndorff.

7. King Kong Bundy set a WWE record with his quick victory at *WrestleMania*. What was the official time of the match?
   a. 7 seconds
   b. 8 seconds
   c. 9 seconds
   d. 10 seconds

8. Whom did Wendi Richter defeat to become WWE Women's Champion at *WrestleMania*?
   a. Leilani Kai
   b. Fabulous Moolah
   c. Rockin' Robin
   d. Cyndi Lauper

9. Who entered the first *WrestleMania* as Intercontinental Champion?
   a. Tito Santana
   b. Rick Steamboat
   c. Don Muraco
   d. Greg Valentine

10. Who managed Big John Studd for his match against Andre the Giant?
    a. Jimmy Hart
    b. Bobby Heenan
    c. Slick
    d. "Classy" Freddie Blassie

WRESTLEMANIA 2

1. *WrestleMania 2* took place in three locations. Which was *not* a site for *WrestleMania 2*?
    a. Los Angeles Memorial Sports Arena
    b. Rosemont Horizon
    c. Philadelphia Spectrum
    d. Nassau Coliseum

2. What LA sports personality was a guest ring announcer at *WrestleMania 2*?
    a. Steve Garvey
    b. Pat Riley
    c. Marcel Dionne
    d. Tommy Lasorda

3. What rock legend accompanied the British Bulldogs to the ring for their Tag Team Championship match at *WrestleMania 2*?
    a. Ozzie Osbourne
    b. Ted Nugent
    c. Alice Cooper
    d. David Bowie

4. Who was Brutus Beefcake's tag team partner in the Dream Team?
    a. Dino Bravo
    b. Honky Tonk Man
    c. Greg Valentine
    d. Tony Atlas

5. In what round of the Mr. T–Roddy Piper boxing match was the fight stopped?
    a. third
    b. fourth
    c. fifth
    d. sixth

6. Who sang "America the Beautiful" at the start of
   WrestleMania 2?
   a. Ray Charles   c. Robert Goulet
   b. Aretha Franklin   d. Cyndi Lauper

7. Who defeated Nikolai Volkoff in a Flag match at
   WrestleMania 2?
   a. Sgt. Slaughter   c. Corp. Kirschner
   b. Jim Duggan   d. Koko B. Ware

8. Who challenged the Fabulous Moolah for the WWE
   Women's Championship at *WrestleMania 2?*
   a. Wendi Richter   c. Rockin' Robin
   b. Sensational Sherri   d. Velvet McIntyre

9. Who faced "Macho Man" Randy Savage for the
   Intercontinental Championship at *WrestleMania 2?*
   a. Rick Steamboat   c. Hillbilly Jim
   b. Greg Valentine   d. George Steele

10. Who managed the Funk Brothers in their match against
    Junkyard Dog and Tito Santana at *WrestleMania 2?*
    a. Bobby Heenan   c. "Classy" Freddie Blassie
    b. Johnny Valiant   d. Jimmy Hart

WRESTLEMANIA III

1. Who teamed with the British Bulldogs for their Six-Man Tag Team match against the Hart Foundation & Danny Davis?
   a. George Steele
   b. Koko B. Ware
   c. Tito Santana
   d. Don Muraco

2. Whom did Alice Cooper accompany to the ring at *WrestleMania III*?
   a. Jake Roberts
   b. Roddy Piper
   c. Junkyard Dog
   d. Billy Jack Haynes

3. What city was the host of *WrestleMania III*?
   a. Cleveland
   b. Chicago
   c. Detroit
   d. Indianapolis

4. Who managed Andre the Giant in his main-event championship match against Hulk Hogan?
   a. Jimmy Hart
   b. Slick
   c. Mr. Fuji
   d. Bobby Heenan

5. What did Randy Savage use to injure Rick Steamboat leading into their *WrestleMania III* Intercontinental Championship match?
   a. steel chair
   b. brass knuckles
   c. ring bell
   d. championship belt

6. What tag team won the opening bout at *WrestleMania III*?
   - a. Rockers
   - b. Demolition
   - c. Can-Am Connection
   - d. Killer Bees

7. Who lost a Hair vs. Hair match to Roddy Piper at *WrestleMania III*?
   - a. Hercules
   - b. Brutus Beefcake
   - c. Adrian Adonis
   - d. Greg Valentine

8. Whom did Harley Race defeat in a Loser Bows match at *WrestleMania III*?
   - a. Koko B. Ware
   - b. Hillbilly Jim
   - c. Jim Duggan
   - d. Junkyard Dog

9. Who was the "Am" member of the Can-Am Connection tag team?
   - a. Tom Zenk
   - b. Koko B. Ware
   - c. Jim Powers
   - d. B. Brian Blair

10. What was the record-setting attendance figure at *WrestleMania III*?
    - a. 83,341
    - b. 87,876
    - c. 90,001
    - d. 93,173

WRESTLEMANIA IV

1. Who won the Twenty-man Battle Royal that opened *WrestleMania IV*?
   a. Bad News Brown
   b. Bret Hart
   c. Harley Race
   d. Ken Patera

2. What tag team joined forces with Bobby Heenan for a Six-Man match against the British Bulldogs and Koko B. Ware?
   a. Powers of Pain
   b. Fabulous Rougeau Brothers
   c. Bolsheviks
   d. Islanders

3. Who sang "America the Beautiful" at the opening of *WrestleMania IV*?
   a. Aretha Franklin
   b. Dionne Warwick
   c. Gladys Knight
   d. Donna Summer

4. How many Superstars participated in the WWE Championship tournament held at *WrestleMania IV*?
   a. 8   b. 12   c. 14   d. 16

5. Who was *not* beaten by Randy Savage on his way to winning the Championship tournament at *WrestleMania IV*?
   a. Ted DiBiase
   b. One Man Gang
   c. Butch Reed
   d. Dino Bravo

6. Who was the guest ring announcer for the final match of *WrestleMania IV*?
   - a. Robin Leach
   - b. Bob Uecker
   - c. Pat Sajak
   - d. Donald Trump

7. In what round of the Championship Tournament was Hulk Hogan eliminated?
   - a. first round
   - b. quarterfinals
   - c. semifinals
   - d. finals

8. What team won the Tag Team Championship at *WrestleMania IV*?
   - a. Hart Foundation
   - b. Twin Towers
   - c. Demolition
   - d. Powers of Pain

9. Who made his *WrestleMania* debut at *WrestleMania IV*, defeating Hercules Hernandez?
   - a. Ultimate Warrior
   - b. Sam Houston
   - c. Ronnie Garvin
   - d. Big Boss Man

10. Who challenged the Honky Tonk Man for the Intercontinental Championship at *WrestleMania IV*?
    - a. Ultimate Warrior
    - b. Jake Roberts
    - c. Brutus Beefcake
    - d. Tito Santana

WRESTLEMANIA V

1. In what state was *WrestleMania V* held?
   - a. New York
   - b. New Jersey
   - c. Pennsylvania
   - d. Massachusetts

2. What controversial talk-show figure was a guest on *Piper's Pit* at *WrestleMania V*?
   - a. Geraldo Rivera
   - b. Jerry Springer
   - c. Joan Rivers
   - d. Morton Downey Jr.

3. Who was the special guest referee for Jake Roberts vs. Andre the Giant?
   - a. Hillbilly Jim
   - b. Hercules
   - c. Big John Studd
   - d. Jesse Ventura

4. Who was in Bobby Heenan's corner for his *WrestleMania V* match against the Red Rooster?
   - a. Brooklyn Brawler
   - b. Dino Bravo
   - c. Arn Anderson
   - d. Mr. Perfect

5. Who entered *WrestleMania V* as the Intercontinental Champion?
   - a. Rick Rude
   - b. Honky Tonk Man
   - c. Mr. Perfect
   - d. Ultimate Warrior

6. Whom did Bad News Brown fight to a no contest at
   WrestleMania V?
   a. Tito Santana   c. Roddy Piper
   b. Jim Duggan   d. Brutus Beefcake

7. Who accompanied Dino Bravo to the ring in
   WrestleMania V?
   a. Earthquake   c. Frenchy Martin
   b. Jimmy Hart   d. Slick

8. How did the Rockers versus Twin Towers match end at
   WrestleMania V?
   a. Akeem pinned Shawn Michaels.
   b. Big Boss Man pinned Marty Jannetty.
   c. Double countout.
   d. Twin Towers were disqualified.

9. What position did Miss Elizabeth take for the WWE
   Championship match at *WrestleMania V*?
   a. In Randy Savage's corner   c. In a neutral corner
   b. In Hulk Hogan's corner   d. She stayed away

10. Who left *WrestleMania V* as the WWE Tag Team
    Champions?
    a. Hart Foundation   c. Powers of Pain
    b. Demolition   d. Brain Busters

WRESTLEMANIA VI

1. Who accompanied Mr. Perfect to the ring for his match with Brutus Beefcake?
   - a. Bobby Heenan
   - b. Rick Rude
   - c. Genius
   - d. Coach

2. Who defeated Andre the Giant & Haku to win the WWE Tag-Team Championship at *WrestleMania VI*?
   - a. Hart Foundation
   - b. Demolition
   - c. Rockers
   - d. Strike Force

3. Who opened *WrestleMania VI* with a rendition of "O Canada"?
   - a. Celine Dion
   - b. Bryan Adams
   - c. Robert Goulet
   - d. Geddy Lee

4. What color was the Cadillac that brought the Honky Tonk Man and Greg Valentine to the ring at *WrestleMania VI*?
   - a. powder blue
   - b. black
   - c. white
   - d. pink

5. What submission maneuver did Rick Martel use to win his match against Koko B. Ware at *WrestleMania VI*?
   - a. Boston Crab
   - b. figure-four leglock
   - c. sleeper hold
   - d. STF

6. The Orient Express defeated the Rockers at *WrestleMania VI*. Who was Tanaka's partner in the Orient Express for the match?

   a. Fuji
   b. Sato
   c. Kato
   d. Haito

7. Bobby Heenan managed the Barbarian at *WrestleMania VI*. Which manager sold Barbarian's contract to Heenan?

   a. Mr. Fuji
   b. Slick
   c. Jimmy Hart
   d. Frenchie Martin

8. Who did Rick Rude defeat at *WrestleMania VI*?

   a. Tito Santana
   b. Jim Duggan
   c. Jimmy Snuka
   d. Roddy Piper

9. What name was given to both *WrestleMania VI* and the main event match between Hulk Hogan and the Ultimate Warrior?

   a. Championship Challenge
   b. Ultimate Challenge
   c. When Worlds Collide
   d. Dream Matchup

10. What was the result of the mixed-tag match between Dusty Rhodes & Sapphire vs. Randy Savage & Queen Sherri?

    a. Rhodes pinned Savage.
    b. Savage pinned Rhodes.
    c. Sapphire pinned Sherri.
    d. Sherri pinned Sapphire.

WRESTLEMANIA VII

1. What city played host to *WrestleMania VII*?
   a. Los Angeles
   c. Phoenix
   b. Las Vegas
   d. San Francisco

2. Who accompanied Big Boss Man to the ring for his Intercontinental Championship match against Mr. Perfect?
   a. Akeem
   c. British Bulldog
   b. Andre the Giant
   d. Koko B. Ware

3. Who was the guest ring announcer for the main event of *WrestleMania VII*?
   a. Pat Sajak
   c. Alex Trebek
   b. Bert Reynolds
   d. Bob Uecker

4. Who made his *WrestleMania* debut at *WrestleMania VII*, pinning "Superfly" Jimmy Snuka?
   a. Ric Flair
   c. Razor Ramon
   b. Undertaker
   d. Yokozuna

5. Who was forced into retirement due to the stipulations of his match at *WrestleMania VII*?
   a. Randy Savage
   c. Jimmy Snuka
   b. Texas Tornado
   d. Sgt. Slaughter

6. Who were the WWE Tag Team Champions heading in to
   WrestleMania VII?
   - a. Nasty Boys
   - b. Legion of Doom
   - c. Demolition
   - d. Hart Foundation

7. How did British Bulldog defeat Warlord at
   WrestleMania VII?
   - a. pinfall
   - b. submission
   - c. disqualification
   - d. countout

8. In what type of match did Jake Roberts and Rick Martel
   compete at *WrestleMania VII?*
   - a. First Blood
   - b. Tuxedo
   - c. Blindfold
   - d. Dog Collar

9. At *WrestleMania VII,* who was the manager of Power
   & Glory?
   - a. Slick
   - b. Jimmy Hart
   - c. Mr. Fuji
   - d. Bobby Heenan

10. Whom did Roddy Piper accompany to the ring for his
    WrestleMania VII match?
    - a. Tito Santana
    - b. Ultimate Warrior
    - c. Hulk Hogan
    - d. Virgil

WRESTLEMANIA VIII

1. Whom did Owen Hart defeat at *WrestleMania VIII*?
   a. Repo Man
   b. Brooklyn Brawler
   c. Doink the Clown
   d. Skinner

2. What legendary manager appeared at *WrestleMania VIII* with the Legion of Doom?
   a. Jim Cornette
   b. J. J. Dillon
   c. Capt. Lou Albano
   d. Paul Ellering

3. Who ran in to help Sid Justice double-team Hulk Hogan at the end of *WrestleMania VIII*?
   a. Ric Flair
   b. Papa Shango
   c. Lex Luger
   d. Jeff Jarrett

4. When Virgil, Big Boss Man, Sgt. Slaughter, and Jim Duggan defeated the Nasty Boys, Repo Man, and the Mountie in an Eight-Man Tag match at *WrestleMania VIII*, who pinned Nasty Boy Knobbs?
   a. Virgil
   b. Big Boss Man
   c. Sgt. Slaughter
   d. Jim Duggan

5. Who won the Intercontinental Championship at *WrestleMania VIII*?
   a. Shawn Michaels
   b. Bret Hart
   c. Roddy Piper
   d. Kerry Von Erich

6. Who managed Sid Justice for his main-event match with Hulk Hogan at *WrestleMania VIII*?
   a. Bobby Heenan
   b. Mr. Fuji
   c. Paul Bearer
   d. Harvey Wippleman

7. Who defeated Rick Martel at *WrestleMania VIII*?
   a. Jake Roberts
   b. Tatanka
   c. Greg Valentine
   d. British Bulldog

8. Who were the WWE Tag Team Champions heading in to *WrestleMania VIII*?
   a. Natural Disasters
   b. Legion of Doom
   c. Money Inc.
   d. Beverly Brothers

9. Who accompanied Ric Flair to the ring for his Championship match against Randy Savage?
   a. Bobby Heenan
   b. Razor Ramon
   c. Ultimate Warrior
   d. Mr. Perfect

10. *WrestleMania VIII* was held in the Hoosier Dome. How many of the previous seven *WrestleMania*s had been held in domed stadiums?
    a. 1   b. 2   c. 3   d. 4

WRESTLEMANIA IX

1. What was the name of the tag team formed by Hulk
    Hogan and Brutus Beefcake that challenged for the Tag
    Team Championship at *WrestleMania IX*?
    - a. Mega Powers
    - b. Hulkamaniacs
    - c. Mega Maniacs
    - d. Super Powers

2. What announcer made his debut at *WrestleMania IX*?
    - a. Gorilla Monsoon
    - b. Jerry Lawler
    - c. Jim Ross
    - d. Michael Cole

3. Who accompanied the Headshrinkers to the ring for their
    match with the Steiner Brothers?
    - a. Afa
    - b. Sika
    - c. High Chief Pete Maivia
    - d. Haku

4. Who did Sensational Sherri accompany to the ring at
    WrestleMania IX?
    - a. Shawn Michaels
    - b. Rick Martel
    - c. Marty Jannetty
    - d. Tatanka

5. What former World Champion did Razor Ramon defeat at
    WrestleMania IX?
    - a. Sgt. Slaughter
    - b. Harley Race
    - c. Bob Backlund
    - d. Ric Flair

6. What city played host to *WrestleMania IX*?
   - a. Chicago
   - b. Houston
   - c. Las Vegas
   - d. New York

7. Who was the Intercontinental Champion heading in to *WrestleMania IX*?
   - a. Razor Ramon
   - b. Shawn Michaels
   - c. Marty Jannetty
   - d. Crush

8. How did the Mr. Perfect–Lex Luger match at *WrestleMania IX* end?
   - a. Mr. Perfect pinned Lex Luger.
   - b. Lex Luger pinned Mr. Perfect.
   - c. Both men were counted out.
   - d. Both men were disqualified.

9. Whom did Undertaker defeat at *WrestleMania IX*?
   - a. King Kong Bundy
   - b. Jake Roberts
   - c. Giant Gonzales
   - d. Bam Bam Bigelow

10. What color were the ring ropes at *WrestleMania IX*?
   - a. red, white, and blue
   - b. black and white
   - c. purple and orange
   - d. black and gold

WRESTLEMANIA X

1. In what type of match did Crush and Randy Savage compete at *WrestleMania X*?
   a. Submission
   b. Blindfold
   c. Falls Count Anywhere
   d. Lumberjack

2. Who managed the Quebecers for their *WrestleMania X* match?
   a. Jimmy Hart
   b. Johnny Polo
   c. Luna Vachon
   d. Jim Cornette

3. Whom did Earthquake face at *WrestleMania X*?
   a. Ludvig Borga
   b. Adam Bomb
   c. Jeff Jarrett
   d. Tatanka

4. Who was the special guest referee for the Lex Luger–Yokozuna WWE Championship match?
   a. Roddy Piper
   b. Owen Hart
   c. Diesel
   d. Mr. Perfect

5. Who sang "American the Beautiful" before *WrestleMania X*?
   a. Reba McEntire
   b. Salt-N-Pepa
   c. Little Richard
   d. Ray Charles

6. Who wrestled in the first and last matches at
   WrestleMania X?
   a. Yokozuna
   b. Shawn Michaels
   c. Bret Hart
   d. Lex Luger

7. What arena was the host of *WrestleMania X*?
   a. Madison Square Garden
   b. The Spectrum
   c. Boston Garden
   d. Rosemont Horizon

8. Who left *WrestleMania X* as the Women's Champion?
   a. Leilani Kai
   b. Luna Vashon
   c. Sensational Sherri
   d. Alundra Blayze

9. Who combined with Mabel & Oscar to make up the tag
   team MOM (Men on a Mission)?
   a. Mike
   b. Mo
   c. Manny
   d. Martin

10. Who was the guest referee for the Bret Hart–Yokozuna
    WWE Championship match?
    a. Roddy Piper
    b. Owen Hart
    c. Diesel
    d. Mr. Perfect

WRESTLEMANIA XI

1. Larry Young, the guest referee in the Undertaker–King Kong Bundy match at *WrestleMania XI*, was better known as an official of what league?
   a. NBA
   b. NFL
   c. NHL
   d. MLB

2. Which NFL player did *not* accompany Lawrence Taylor to the ring for his match with Bam Bam Bigelow at *WrestleMania XI*?
   a. Carl Banks
   b. Andre Tippett
   c. Reggie White
   d. Steve McMichael

3. Who was in Razor Ramon's corner for his Intercontinental Championship match against Jeff Jarrett?
   a. Diesel
   b. Triple H
   c. Shawn Michaels
   d. 1-2-3 Kid

4. Who escorted Diesel to the ring for his WWE Championship defense at *WrestleMania XI*?
   a. Jenny McCarthy
   b. Jennie Garth
   c. Pamela Anderson
   d. Cindy Crawford

5. In what type of match did Bret Hart and Bob Backlund compete at *WrestleMania XI*?
   a. Submission
   b. Steel Cage
   c. "I Quit"
   d. Falls Count Anywhere

6. Who won the WWE Tag Team Championship at
    WrestleMania XI?
    a. Lex Luger & British Bulldog
    b. Smokin' Guns
    c. Owen Hart & Yokuzuna
    d. Blu Brothers

7. Who accompanied the Blu Brothers to the ring for their
    match with Lex Luger & the British Bulldog?
    a. Hillbilly Jim   c. Uncle Zebekiah
    b. Uncle Elmer   d. Roadie

8. Who was the guest referee for the Bret Hart–Bob Backlund
    match at *WrestleMania XI*?
    a. Mr. Perfect   c. Roddy Piper
    b. Ted DiBiase   d. 1-2-3 Kid

9. What state played host to *WrestleMania XI*?
    a. New York   c. Connecticut
    b. Pennsylvania   d. Massachusetts

10. What Salt-N-Pepa hit served as Lawrence Taylor's entrance
    music?
    a. "Push It"   c. "The Show Stopper"
    b. "Whatta Man"   d. "Shake Your Thang"

WRESTLEMANIA XII

1. Who ordered the main event match between Bret Hart and Shawn Michaels into overtime when it was tied at the end of sixty minutes?
   a. Roddy Piper
   b. Mr. McMahon
   c. Gorilla Monsoon
   d. Jim Ross

2. Who got the pin when Jim Cornette's team defeated Yokozuna, Jake Roberts, and Ahmed Johnson?
   a. Jim Cornette
   b. Vader
   c. Owen Hart
   d. British Bulldog

3. Whom did Stone Cold Steve Austin defeat at *WrestleMania XII*, his *WrestleMania* debut?
   a. Ted DiBiase
   b. Henry Godwinn
   c. Razor Ramon
   d. Savio Vega

4. Who accompanied Triple H to the ring for his *WrestleMania XII* match against the Ultimate Warrior?
   a. Sable
   b. Chyna
   c. Sunny
   d. Stephanie McMahon

5. Whom did Undertaker defeat at *WrestleMania XII*?
   a. Razor Ramon
   b. Diesel
   c. Sid
   d. Kane

6. What team won the WWE Tag Team Championship on the Free-For-All leading in to *WrestleMania XII*?
   a. Godwinns
   b. Smokin' Gunns
   c. Headbangers
   d. Bodydonnas

7. What California city played host to *WrestleMania XII*?
   a. San Jose
   b. San Diego
   c. Anaheim
   d. Los Angeles

8. How did Roddy Piper win the Hollywood Backlot Brawl against Goldust at *WrestleMania XII*?
   a. He pinned Goldust.
   b. Goldust submitted to the sleeper hold.
   c. He stripped Goldust down, and Goldust walked out.
   d. Goldust was disqualified for giving Piper the Shattered Dreams.

9. What manager accompanied Yokozuna, Jake Roberts, and Ahmed Johnson to the ring for their match against Jim Cornette's team?
   a. Mr. Fuji
   b. Jimmy Hart
   c. Bobby Heenan
   d. Harvey Whippleman

10. What move did Steve Austin use to finish off his opponent at *WrestleMania XII*?
    a. stun gun
    b. Thesz press
    c. Stone Cold stunner
    d. Million Dollar Dream

WRESTLEMANIA 13

1. Who was the special guest referee for the Bret Hart–Steve Austin match at *WrestleMania 13*?
    a. Ken Shamrock
    b. Roddy Piper
    c. Shawn Michaels
    d. Mr. Perfect

2. Which was the first team eliminated in the Four-Way Tag Team Elimination match at *WrestleMania 13*?
    a. Headbangers
    b. Godwinns
    c. New Blackjacks
    d. Doug Furnas & Phil Lafon

3. Who teamed with Mankind to challenge Owen Hart and the British Bulldog for the WWE Tag Team Championship?
    a. Goldust
    b. Vader
    c. Terry Funk
    d. Flash Funk

4. In what type of match did Undertaker and Sycho Sid compete for the WWE Championship at *WrestleMania 13*?
    a. Steel Cage
    b. No-Disqualification
    c. Street Fight
    d. Submission

5. Who was *not* on the Nation of Domination team that competed in a Six-Man Chicago Street Fight at *WrestleMania 13*?
    a. D'Lo Brown
    b. Faarooq
    c. Savio Vega
    d. Crush

6. What was the last *WrestleMania* before *13* not to use a Roman numeral in its title?

   a. 2   b. 4   c. 7   d. 9

7. Who was the Intercontinental Champion heading in to *WrestleMania 13*?

   a. Sultan   c. Billy Gunn
   b. Triple H   d. The Rock

8. Who teamed with the Legion of Doom for their six-man Chicago Street Fight against the Nation of Domination?

   a. Droz   c. Ahmed Johnson
   b. Jake Roberts   d. Billy Gunn

9. What city played host to *WrestleMania 13*?

   a. Detroit   c. Philadelphia
   b. Minneapolis   d. Chicago

10. What former Intercontinental Champion did guest commentary during the Intercontinental Championship match at *WrestleMania 13*?

   a. Randy Savage   c. Honky Tonk Man
   b. Roddy Piper   d. Mr. Perfect

WRESTLEMANIA XIV

1. What team won the fifteen-team Battle Royal at
    WrestleMania XIV?
    a. Godwinns   c. Rock 'n' Roll Express
    b. LOD 2000   d. Quebecers

2. How did the mixed tag of Marc Mero & Sable vs. Goldust &
    Luna Vachon end at *WrestleMania XIV?*
    a. Mero pinned Goldust. c. Sable pinned Luna.
    b. Goldust pinned Mero. d. Luna pinned Sable.

3. Whom was Chyna handcuffed to during the European
    Championship match between Triple H and Owen Hart
    at *WrestleMania XIV?*
    a. Stu Hart   c. Bob Backlund
    b. Sgt. Slaughter   d. Roddy Piper

4. In what type of match did the New Age Outlaws
    and Cactus Jack & Chainsaw Charlie compete at
    WrestleMania XIV?
    a. Steel Cage   c. Dumpster
    b. Ladder   d. Tables

5. What sports star served as special guest ring announcer
    for the Undertaker-Kane match at *WrestleMania XIV?*
    a. Lawrence Taylor   c. Deion Sanders
    b. Joe Thiesman   d. Pete Rose

6. What city played host to *WrestleMania XIV*?
   a. New York   c. Boston
   b. Anaheim   d. Philadelphia

7. Who left *WrestleMania XIV* as the Light Heavyweight Champion?
   a. Aguila   c. Taka Michinoku
   b. X-Pac   d. Essa Rios

8. What was the last team eliminated from the fifteen-team Battle Royal at *WrestleMania XIV*?
   a. Headbangers   c. Truth Commission
   b. New Midnight Express d. Too Much

9. Who left *WrestleMania XIV* as the Intercontinental Champion?
   a. The Rock   c. Jeff Jarrett
   b. Ken Shamrock   d. Bradshaw

10. Who made the three count for Steve Austin's victory over Shawn Michaels for the WWE Championship at *WrestleMania XIV*?
    a. Mick Foley   c. Tim White
    b. Shane McMahon   d. Mike Tyson

WRESTLEMANIA XV

1. Who was the WWE commissioner at *WrestleMania XV*?
   - a. Gorilla Monsoon
   - b. Roddy Piper
   - c. Shawn Michaels
   - d. Sgt. Slaughter

2. Who won the four-man elimination match for the Intercontinental Championship at *WrestleMania XV*?
   - a. Val Venis
   - b. Road Dogg
   - c. Ken Shamrock
   - d. Goldust

3. Who faced Bart Gunn in a Brawl-For-All match at *WrestleMania XV*?
   - a. George Foreman
   - b. Chuck Wepner
   - c. Butterbean
   - d. Evander Holyfield

4. Who left *WrestleMania XV* as the WWE Hardcore Champion?
   - a. Hardcore Holly
   - b. Billy Gunn
   - c. Al Snow
   - d. Crash Holly

5. Who won the match for the right to be the special guest referee in the main event of *WrestleMania XV*?
   - a. Big Show
   - b. Mankind
   - c. Triple H
   - d. British Bulldog

6. What famous mascot did Pete Rose disguise himself as in order to attack Kane at *WrestleMania XV*?

   a. Phillie Phanatic   c. San Diego Chicken
   b. Phoenix Gorilla   d. Syracuse Orange

7. Who accompanied Shane McMahon to the ring for his European Championship match at *WrestleMania XV*?

   a. Stephanie McMahon   c. Pete Gas
   b. Test   d. Gerald Briscoe

8. Who attacked Tori in her WWE Women's Championship match against Sable, allowing Sable to retain the championship?

   a. Jazz   c. Nicole Bass
   b. Jacqueline   d. Ivory

9. In what type of match did Steve Austin and The Rock wrestle for the WWE Championship at *WrestleMania XV*?

   a. Street Fight   c. No Disqualification
   b. Corporate Clash   d. Two-Out-of-Three Falls

10. Who were the Tag Team Champions heading in to *WrestleMania XV*?

    a. Owen Hart & Jeff Jarrett   c. Brood
    b. Test & D'Lo Brown   d. Hardy Boys

WRESTLEMANIA XVI

1. What rap star performed the Godfather's theme music at *WrestleMania XVI*?
   - a. Ice Cube
   - b. Ice-T
   - c. Vanilla Ice
   - d. Dr. Dre

2. Who won the Fatal Four Way Elimination match for the WWE Championship at *WrestleMania XVI*?
   - a. The Rock
   - b. Big Show
   - c. Triple H
   - d. Mick Foley

3. Who won the European Championship at *WrestleMania XVI*?
   - a. Chris Jericho
   - b. Kurt Angle
   - c. Jeff Jarrett
   - d. D'Lo Brown

4. What Superstar recorded two pins during the fifteen-minute Battle Royal for the Hardcore Championship at *WrestleMania XVI*?
   - a. Hardcore Holly
   - b. Tazz
   - c. Crash Holly
   - d. Bradshaw

5. Who was the special guest referee for the Catfight between Terri Runnels and Kat at *WrestleMania XVI*?
   - a. Jerry Lawler
   - b. Hugh Hefner
   - c. Fabulous Moolah
   - d. Val Venis

6. Who was eliminated first from the Four-Way Elimination match for the Championship at *WrestleMania XVI*?
   a. The Rock
   b. Big Show
   c. Triple H
   d. Mick Foley

7. Who won the WWE Tag Team Championship at *WrestleMania XVI*?
   a. Edge & Christian
   b. Hardy Boys
   c. Dudley Boys
   d. D-Generation X

8. Who got the pin when Too Cool & Chyna defeated the Radicalz at *WrestleMania XVI*?
   a. Scotty 2 Hotty
   b. Grandmaster Sexay
   c. Rikishi
   d. Chyna

9. What was the name of the tag team featuring Al Snow & Steve Blackman that faced Test & Albert at *WrestleMania XVI*?
   a. Ultimate Fighting
   b. J.O.B. Squad
   c. Head Cheese
   d. Hardcore Legends

10. Who left *WrestleMania XVI* as the Hardcore Champion?
    a. Hardcore Holly
    b. Tazz
    c. Crash Holly
    d. Bradshaw

WRESTLEMANIA X-SEVEN

1. Who won the Gimmick Battle Royal at *WrestleMania X-Seven*?

   a. Hillbilly Jim
   b. Sgt. Slaughter
   c. Earthquake
   d. Iron Sheik

2. Who did *not* interfere in the three-way TLC match among the Hardys, Dudleys, and Edge & Christian at *WrestleMania X-Seven*?

   a. Lita
   b. Sign Guy Dudley
   c. Spike Dudley
   d. Rhyno

3. Who won the WWE Women's Championship at *WrestleMania X-Seven*?

   a. Ivory
   b. Chyna
   c. Trish Stratus
   d. Lita

4. Who won the European Championship at *WrestleMania X-Seven*?

   a. Test
   b. William Regal
   c. Eddie Guerrero
   d. Perry Saturn

5. Who won the Hardcore Championship at *WrestleMania X-Seven*?

   a. Raven
   b. Big Show
   c. Big Boss Man
   d. Kane

6. Who was the special guest referee when Vince McMahon and Shane McMahon met at *WrestleMania X-Seven*?
   a. Linda McMahon
   b. Shawn Michaels
   c. Mick Foley
   d. Ric Flair

7. What move did Undertaker use to defeat Triple H at *WrestleMania X-Seven*?
   a. Tombstone
   b. Last Ride
   c. Old School
   d. Dragon sleeper

8. Who interfered on Steve Austin's behalf in his WWE Championship match against The Rock at *WrestleMania X-Seven*?
   a. Mick Foley
   b. Triple H
   c. Undertaker
   d. Mr. McMahon

9. What was the tagline for *WrestleMania X-Seven*?
   a. Rocketing the WWE in a New Direction
   b. Houston . . . We Have a Problem
   c. The Attitude Era Reborn
   d. The One and Only

10. Who won the WWE Tag Team Championship at *WrestleMania X-Seven*?
    a. Edge & Christian
    b. Hardy Boys
    c. Dudley Boys
    d. APA

WRESTLEMANIA X8

1. Who left *WrestleMania X8* as the European Champion?
   a. Christian
   b. William Regal
   c. Mr. Perfect
   d. Diamond Dallas Page

2. How many times did the WWE Hardcore Championship change hands at *WrestleMania X8*?
   a. 3   b. 5   c. 7   d. 9

3. Who won the Triple-Threat match for the Women's Championship at *WrestleMania X8*?
   a. Lita
   b. Victoria
   c. Trish Stratus
   d. Jazz

4. Whom did Kurt Angle defeat at *WrestleMania X8*?
   a. Shawn Michaels
   b. Kevin Nash
   c. Kane
   d. Brock Lesnar

5. Who won the Four Corners Elimination match for the Tag Team Championship at *WrestleMania X8*?
   a. APA
   b. Hardy Boys
   c. Dudley Boys
   d. Billy & Chuck

6. Who tried to help Ric Flair by interfering in his match against Undertaker at *WrestleMania X8*?
   a. Dusty Rhodes
   b. Arn Anderson
   c. David Flair
   d. Roddy Piper

7. Who entered *WrestleMania X8* as Intercontinental Champion?
   a. William Regal
   b. Christian
   c. Rob Van Dam
   d. Booker T

8. Who accompanied Chris Jericho to the ring for his Undisputed Championship match at *WrestleMania X8*?
   a. Lance Storm
   b. Christian
   c. Stephanie McMahon
   d. Test

9. What member of the nWo did Steve Austin face at *WrestleMania X8*?
   a. Kevin Nash
   b. Scott Hall
   c. X-Pac
   d. Big Show

10. What city played host to *WrestleMania X8*?
    a. Houston
    b. Seattle
    c. Toronto
    d. Indianapolis

WRESTLEMANIA XIX

1. What city played host to *WrestleMania XIX*?
   a. Philadelphia
   b. Seattle
   c. Houston
   d. Chicago

2. How many Rock Bottoms did The Rock deliver to Steve Austin before he pinned him at *WrestleMania XIX*?
   a. 1
   b. 2
   c. 3
   d. 4

3. What former rival of Hulk Hogan interfered on
    Mr. McMahon's behalf during the Hulk Hogan–
    Mr. McMahon Street Fight?
    a. Ric Flair   c. King Kong Bundy
    b. Roddy Piper   d. Ted DiBiase

4. Who left *WrestleMania XIX* as WWE Champion?
    a. Kurt Angle   c. Brock Lesnar
    b. Eddie Guerrero   d. Goldberg

5. Against whom did Triple H defend the World Heavyweight
    Championship at *WrestleMania XIX*?
    a. Rob Van Dam   c. Booker T
    b. Kane   d. Shawn Michaels

6. Who entered *WrestleMania XIX* as Cruiserweight
    Champion?
    a. Rey Mysterio   c. Shannon Moore
    b. Chavo Guerrero   d. Matt Hardy

7. What type of match did the Miller Lite Catfight girls have
    with Stacy Keibler and Torrie Wilson at *WrestleMania XIX*?
    a. Bra and Panties   c. Pillow Fight
    b. Dance Off   d. Water Balloon Fight

8. Who was scheduled to be Undertaker's partner against Big
    Show and A-Train at *WrestleMania XIX*?
    a. Kane   c. Scott Steiner
    b. Nathan Jones   d. Vader

9. Who accompanied Triple H to the ring for his match at
   WrestleMania XIX?
   a. Stephanie McMahon   c. Shawn Michaels
   b. Ric Flair   d. Randy Orton

10. Who won the WWE Women's Championship at
    WrestleMania XIX?
    a. Victoria   c. Trish Stratus
    b. Jazz   d. Lita

WRESTLEMANIA XX

1. For what championship did John Cena wrestle at
   WrestleMania XX?
   a. WWE   c. Intercontinental
   b. World Heavyweight   d. United States

2. Who got the win for Evolution in their handicap match
   against the Rock 'n' Sock Connection at *WrestleMania XX*?
   a. Randy Orton   c. Ric Flair
   b. Batista   d. Triple H

3. What team won the Fatal Four Way match for the Tag
   Team Championship at *WrestleMania XX*?
   a. APA
   b. Basham Brothers
   c. Rikishi & Scotty 2 Hotty
   d. World's Greatest Tag Team

4. What Diva had her head shaved at *WrestleMania XX*?

   a. Victoria
   b. Lita
   c. Molly Holly
   d. Gail Kim

5. Who was the WWE Champion going in to *WrestleMania XX*?

   a. Kurt Angle
   b. John Cena
   c. Shawn Michaels
   d. Eddie Guerrero

6. Who won the Cruiserweight Open at *WrestleMania XX*?

   a. Billy Kidman
   b. Chavo Guerrero
   c. Jamie Noble
   d. Rey Mysterio

7. Who was the World Heavyweight Champion entering *WrestleMania XX*?

   a. Undertaker
   b. Triple H
   c. Shawn Michaels
   d. Kurt Angle

8. What controversial figure did Jesse Ventura interview at *WrestleMania XX*?

   a. Hillary Clinton
   b. Al Sharpton
   c. Donald Trump
   d. Rosie O'Donnell

9. Whom did Undertaker defeat at *WrestleMania XX*?

   a. JBL
   b. Kane
   c. Big Show
   d. Mankind

10. What was the outcome of the Goldberg–Brock Lesnar match at *WrestleMania XX*?
    a. Lesnar pinned Goldberg.
    b. Goldberg pinned Lesnar.
    c. Both men were disqualified.
    d. Both men were counted out.

WRESTLEMANIA 21

1. What Superstar faced Akebono in a Sumo match at *WrestleMania 21*?
    a. Viscera
    b. Rikishi
    c. Umaga
    d. Big Show

2. Who was *not* a participant in the Money in the Bank Ladder match at *WrestleMania 21*?
    a. Christian
    b. Jericho
    c. Rhyno
    d. Shelton Benjamin

3. Who saved Eugene from being double-teamed by Muhammad Hassan and Daivari at *WrestleMania 21*?
    a. Hulk Hogan
    b. Jim Duggan
    c. Ric Flair
    d. Mick Foley

4. Who was Roddy Piper's guest on *The Piper's Pit* that was part of *WrestleMania 21*?
    a. Hulk Hogan
    b. Paul Orndorff
    c. Steve Austin
    d. Carlito

5. Whom did Christy Hemme challenge for the Women's Championship at *WrestleMania 21*?
   a. Lita
   b. Trish Stratus
   c. Victoria
   d. Torrie Wilson

6. What WWE Legend inspired Randy Orton to challenge Undertaker at *WrestleMania 21*?
   a. Bob Orton
   b. Jake Roberts
   c. Superstar Billy Graham
   d. Don Muraco

7. Who performed Triple H's entrance theme live prior to his match at *WrestleMania 21*?
   a. Motörhead
   b. Drowning Pool
   c. P.O.D.
   d. Metallica

8. The opening to *WrestleMania 21* featured Steve Austin in a parody of what film?
   a. *Terminator*
   b. *Gladiator*
   c. *Dirty Harry*
   d. *Rear Window*

9. Whom did Rey Mysterio defeat in the opening match at *WrestleMania 21*?
   a. Edge
   b. Matt Hardy
   c. Hurricane
   d. Eddie Guerrero

10. Who was the WWE Champion heading in to *WrestleMania 21*?
   a. Triple H
   b. Batista
   c. Shawn Michaels
   d. JBL

WRESTLEMANIA 22

1. What was the official *WrestleMania 22* slogan?
   - a. Big Time
   - b. All Grown Up
   - c. Feel the Heat
   - d. Clash of the Immortals

2. Who won the United States Championship at *WrestleMania 22*?
   - a. MVP
   - b. JBL
   - c. Johnny Nitro
   - d. Chavo Guerrero

3. Who won the Money in the Bank Ladder match at *WrestleMania 22*?
   - a. Ric Flair
   - b. Matt Hardy
   - c. Rob Van Dam
   - d. Shelton Benjamin

4. Who was the WWE Women's Champion entering *WrestleMania 22*?
   - a. Mickie James
   - b. Trish Stratus
   - c. Lita
   - d. Victoria

5. Who sang "America the Beautiful" at the beginning of *WrestleMania 22*?
   - a. Michelle Williams
   - b. Kelly Rowland
   - c. Kelly Clarkson
   - d. Aretha Franklin

6. What city played host to *WrestleMania 22*?
   - a. Detroit
   - b. Los Angeles
   - c. New York
   - d. Chicago

7. Who was *not* a part of the Triple-Threat match for the World Heavyweight Championship at *WrestleMania 22*?
   a. Kurt Angle
   b. JBL
   c. Randy Orton
   d. Rey Mysterio

8. What Diva won the Playboy Pillow Fight at *WrestleMania 22*?
   a. Maria
   b. Candice Michelle
   c. Torrie Wilson
   d. Ashley

9. In what type of match did Undertaker and Mark Henry fight at *WrestleMania 22*?
   a. Casket
   b. Buried Alive
   c. Last Ride
   d. Hell in a Cell

10. Who challenged John Cena for the WWE Championship at *WrestleMania 22*?
   a. Shawn Michaels
   b. Kurt Angle
   c. Edge
   d. Triple H

WRESTLEMANIA 23

1. Who was *not* in the Money in the Bank match at *WrestleMania 23*?
   a. Matt Hardy
   b. Finlay
   c. Shelton Benjamin
   d. Edge

2. For what championship did MVP compete at
   WrestleMania 23?
   a. United States
   b. Intercontinental
   c. Cruiserweight
   d. ECW

3. Who won the Money in the Bank Ladder match at
   WrestleMania 23?
   a. Edge
   b. Randy Orton
   c. Jeff Hardy
   d. Mr. Kennedy

4. Who got the pin when the ECW Originals faced the New
   Breed at *WrestleMania 23*?
   a. Sabu
   b. Sandman
   c. Rob Van Dam
   d. Tommy Dreamer

5. In what type of match did Ashley and Melina compete for
   the WWE Women's Championship at *WrestleMania 23*?
   a. Bra and Panties
   b. Playboy Pillow Fight
   c. Lady Ladder
   d. Lumberjill

6. Who was the official special guest referee for the Bobby
   Lashley–Umaga match?
   a. Shane McMahon
   b. Steve Austin
   c. Mr. McMahon
   d. Mick Foley

7. What move did John Cena use to win his match against
   Shawn Michaels at *WrestleMania 23*?
   a. F-U
   b. powerbomb
   c. STFU
   d. five knuckle shuffle

8. Who was *not* a member of the New Breed team at *WrestleMania 23*?
    a. Miz
    b. Matt Striker
    c. Kevin Thorn
    d. Elijah Burke

9. In what Detroit-area venue was *WrestleMania 23* held?
    a. Comerica Park
    b. Silverdome
    c. Palace at Auburn Hills
    d. Ford Field

10. Whom did Great Khali defeat at *WrestleMania 23*?
    a. Ric Flair
    b. Carlito
    c. Kane
    d. Batista

SECTION V
BACKLASH

BACKLASH 1999–2000

1. What two former members of D-Generation X faced each other at *Backlash 1999*?
   a. Triple H and X-Pac
   b. Triple H and Billy Gunn
   c. Triple H and Road Dogg
   d. Triple H and Chyna

2. Who was the special guest referee when Steve Austin and The Rock wrestled for the WWE Championship at *Backlash 1999*?
   a. Shane McMahon
   b. Ken Shamrock
   c. Shawn Michaels
   d. Roddy Piper

3. In what type of match did Mankind and Big Show compete at *Backlash 1999*?
   a. Brass Knuckles on a Pole
   b. First Blood
   c. Boiler Room Brawl
   d. Falls Count Anywhere

4. What Diva accompanied Jeff Jarrett and Owen Hart to the ring for their match at *Backlash 1999*?
   a. Debra
   b. Sable
   c. Lita
   d. Ivory

5. Who was *not* a member of the Ministry of Darkness team that faced the Brood at *Backlash 1999*?
   a. Bradshaw
   b. Faarooq
   c. Mideon
   d. Viscera

6. Who won the WWE Championship at *Backlash 2000*?
   a. Steve Austin
   b. Mankind
   c. The Rock
   d. Triple H

7. For what championship did Eddie Guerrero and Essa Rios compete at *Backlash 2000*?
   a. Light Heavyweight
   b. European
   c. Cruiserweight
   d. United States

8. What Diva did the Dudley Boys powerbomb through a table after their match at *Backlash 2000*?
   a. Mae Young
   b. Kat
   c. Trish Stratus
   d. Terri Runnels

9. Whom did Crash Holly pin in the six-man Hardcore match to retain the Hardcore Championship at *Backlash 2000*?
   a. Perry Saturn
   b. Tazz
   c. Hardcore Holly
   d. Jeff Hardy

10. Who was the WWE Light Heavyweight Champion heading into *Backlash 2000*?
    a. Dean Malenko
    b. Eddie Guerrero
    c. Essa Rios
    d. Scotty 2 Hotty

BACKLASH 2001–2002

1. Who won the Triple-Threat match for the WWE European Championship at *Backlash 2001*?
   a. Eddie Guerrero
   b. Matt Hardy
   c. Christian
   d. Jeff Hardy

2. Who was *not* on the X-Factor team that faced the Dudley Boys and Spike at *Backlash 2001*?
   a. K-Kwik
   b. X-Pac
   c. Albert
   d. Justin Credible

3. Whom did William Regal defeat in a Duchess of Queensbury Rules match at *Backlash 2001*?
   a. Edge
   b. Crash Holly
   c. Chris Jericho
   d. Kurt Angle

4. Who scored the pin when Steve Austin & Triple H met Undertaker & Kane in the main event of *Backlash 2001*?
   a. Steve Austin
   b. Triple H
   c. Undertaker
   d. Kane

5. Who challenged Rhyno for the WWE Hardcore Championship at *Backlash 2001*?
   a. Tommy Dreamer
   b. Jerry Lynn
   c. Raven
   d. Test

6. Who was the special guest referee when Undertaker and Steve Austin met at *Backlash 2002*?
   a. Shane McMahon
   b. Ric Flair
   c. Kevin Nash
   d. Shawn Michaels

7. Who accompanied Tajiri to the ring for his WWE Cruiserweight Championship match at *Backlash 2002*?
   a. Gail Kim
   b. Stacy Keibler
   c. Torrie Wilson
   d. Lita

8. Who retained the WWE Women's Championship at *Backlash 2002*?
   a. Jazz
   b. Victoria
   c. Trish Stratus
   d. Jackie Gayda

9. Who defeated Rob Van Dam for the Intercontinental Championship at *Backlash 2002*?
   a. Edge
   b. Big Show
   c. Eddie Guerrero
   d. Matt Hardy

10. Who interfered in the Hulk Hogan–Triple H match at *Backlash 2002*, allowing Hogan to win the Undisputed WWE Championship?
    a. Mr. McMahon
    b. Undertaker
    c. The Rock
    d. Kevin Nash

BACKLASH 2003

1. Who was the special guest referee when Rob Van Dam &
   Kane challenged the Dudley Boys for the World Tag Team
   Championship at *Backlash 2003*?
   - a. Spike Dudley
   - b. Eric Bischoff
   - c. Jonathan Coachman
   - d. Chief Morley

2. Whom did Goldberg defeat at *Backlash 2003*, his WWE
   Pay-Per-View debut?
   - a. Steve Austin
   - b. Undertaker
   - c. The Rock
   - d. Scott Steiner

3. Who challenged Brock Lesnar for the WWE
   Championship at *Backlash 2003*?
   - a. Kurt Angle
   - b. Randy Orton
   - c. John Cena
   - d. Bradshaw

4. Whom did Roddy Piper accompany to the ring for a match
   with Rikishi at *Backlash 2003*?
   - a. Chuck Palumbo
   - b. Tyson Tomko
   - c. Sean O'Haire
   - d. Heidenreich

5. What was the result of the match that saw Team Angle successfully defend the Tag Team Championship against Los Guerreros at *Backlash 2003*?
   a. Shelton Benjamin pinned Chavo Guerrero.
   b. Shelton Benjamin pinned Eddie Guerrero.
   c. Charlie Haas pinned Chavo Guerrero.
   d. Charlie Haas pinned Eddie Guerrero.

6. Who teamed with Shawn Michaels & Kevin Nash to face the team of Triple H, Ric Flair, and Chris Jericho at *Backlash 2003*?
   a. Scott Hall
   b. Batista
   c. Booker T
   d. Matt Hardy

7. Whom did Jazz defeat to win the WWE Women's Championship at *Backlash 2003*?
   a. Jacqueline
   b. Victoria
   c. Trish Stratus
   d. Sable

8. What was the result of the match featuring teams led by Triple H and Shawn Michaels at *Backlash 2003*?
   a. Triple H pinned Kevin Nash.
   b. Shawn Michaels pinned Ric Flair.
   c. Kevin Nash pinned Chris Jericho.
   d. Chris Jericho pinned Shawn Michaels.

9. Who accompanied Jazz to the ring for her WWE Women's Championship match at *Backlash 2003*?
   a. Rodney Mack
   b. Steven Richards
   c. Theodore Long
   d. Paul Heyman

10. What was the result of the match between Rey Mysterio and Big Show at *Backlash 2003*?
    a. Rey Mysterio pinned Big Show.
    b. Big Show pinned Rey Mysterio.
    c. Rey Mysterio won by disqualification.
    d. The referee stopped the match, declaring Rey Mysterio unable to continue.

BACKLASH 2004–2005

1. Whom did Jonathan Coachman defeat at *Backlash 2004*?
    a. William Regal
    b. Val Venis
    c. Tajiri
    d. Eugene

2. What was the result of the Handicap match that saw Chris Jericho take on the duo of Christian & Trish Stratus at *Backlash 2004*?
    a. Jericho pinned Christian.
    b. Jericho pinned Trish Stratus.
    c. Christian pinned Jericho.
    d. Trish Stratus pinned Jericho.

3. Who successfully defended the WWE Women's Championship at *Backlash 2004*?
    a. Lita
    b. Victoria
    c. Molly Holly
    d. Gail Kim

4. What Superstar defeated Ric Flair at *Backlash 2004*?
   a. Hurricane
   b. Matt Hardy
   c. Shelton Benjamin
   d. Shawn Michaels

5. Who challenged Randy Orton for the Intercontinental Championship in a No Holds Barred, Falls Count Anywhere match at *Backlash 2004*?
   a. Kane
   b. Mick Foley
   c. Edge
   d. Triple H

6. What Superstar faced Kane on behalf of Trish Stratus at *Backlash 2005*?
   a. Chris Masters
   b. Snitsky
   c. Tyson Tomko
   d. Viscera

7. What team won the Tag Team Turmoil match for the World Tag Team Championship at *Backlash 2005*?
   a. Tajiri & William Regal
   b. La Resistance
   c. Hurricane & Rosey
   d. Heart Throbs

8. Who successfully defended the Intercontinental Championship at *Backlash 2005*?
   a. Chris Jericho
   b. Christian
   c. Jeff Hardy
   d. Shelton Benjamin

9. In what type of match did Edge defeat Chris Benoit at *Backlash 2005*?
   a. Ladder
   b. Iron Man
   c. Last Man Standing
   d. Ultimate Submission

10. Who teamed with Hulk Hogan to defeat Muhammad Hassan & Daivari at *Backlash 2005*?

    a. John Cena   c. Triple H
    b. Batista   d. Shawn Michaels

BACKLASH 2006–2007

1. What was the result of the match between Big Show and Kane at *Backlash 2006*?

    a. Kane pinned Big Show.
    b. Big Show pinned Kane.
    c. The match was declared no contest.
    d. Both men were disqualified.

2. What was the result of the tag team match at *Backlash 2006* pitting Mr. McMahon & Shane McMahon against Shawn Michaels & "God"?

    a. Shawn Michaels pinned Shane McMahon.
    b. Shawn Michaels pinned Mr. McMahon.
    c. Mr. McMahon pinned Shawn Michaels.
    d. Shane McMahon pinned Shawn Michaels.

3. Who won the Intercontinental Championship at *Backlash 2006*?

    a. Carlito   c. William Regal
    b. Rob Van Dam   d. Johnny Nitro

4. What was the result of the WWE Women's Championship match between Mickie James and Trish Stratus at *Backlash 2006*?
   a. Mickie James won by pinfall.
   b. The referee ruled Trish Stratus was unable to continue due to injury.
   c. Trish Stratus won by disqualification.
   d. Trish Stratus won by countout.

5. In what type of match did John Cena defend the WWE Championship at *Backlash 2006*?
   a. No Disqualification
   b. Fatal Four Way
   c. Triple Threat
   d. "I Quit"

6. Who got the pin when the Hardys successfully defended the World Tag Team Championship against Lance Cade & Trevor Murdoch at *Backlash 2007*?
   a. Jeff Hardy pinned Lance Cade.
   b. Matt Hardy pinned Lance Cade.
   c. Jeff Hardy pinned Trevor Murdoch.
   d. Matt Hardy pinned Trevor Murdoch.

7. Melina successfully defended the Women's Championship at *Backlash 2007* against what Diva?
   a. Candice
   b. Torrie Wilson
   c. Mickie James
   d. Victoria

8. In what type of match did Undertaker and Batista compete for the World Heavyweight Championship at *Backlash 2007*?

   a. Steel Cage

   b. Falls Count Anywhere

   c. Last Man Standing

   d. Casket

9. Whom did John Cena pin in the Fatal Four Way match for the WWE Championship at *Backlash 2007* to retain his championship?

   a. Shawn Michaels

   b. Randy Orton

   c. Triple H

   d. Edge

10. Who won the ECW Championship at *Backlash 2007*?

    a. Bobby Lashley

    b. CM Punk

    c. Mr. McMahon

    d. Umaga

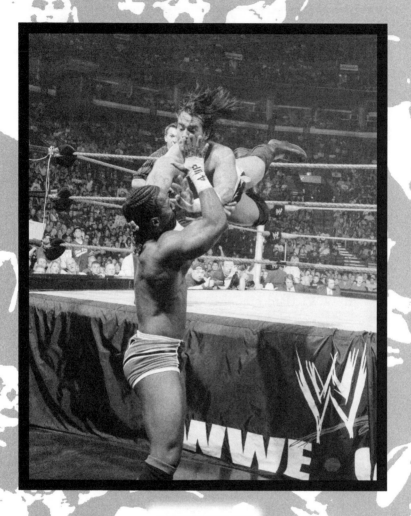

SECTION VI
JUDGMENT DAY

JUDGMENT DAY 1998–2002

1. At the first *Judgment Day* in 1998, Kane and Undertaker fought for the vacant WWE Championship. Who was the special guest referee for the match?
   a. Mankind
   b. The Rock
   c. Steve Austin
   d. Shane McMahon

2. What championship did X-Pac win at *Judgment Day 1998*?
   a. WWE Intercontinental
   b. WWE European
   c. WWE Light Heavyweight
   d. WWE Hardcore

3. Which Superstar did *not* interfere on Shane McMahon's behalf during his match against Big Show at *Judgment Day 2000*?
   a. Bull Buchanan
   b. Albert
   c. Big Boss Man
   d. Ken Shamrock

4. What was the final score of the sixty-minute Iron Man match for the WWE Championship between The Rock and Triple H at *Judgment Day 2000*?
   a. The Rock won 5–4.
   b. Triple H won 3–2.
   c. Triple H won 6–5.
   d. The Rock won 2–1.

5. In what type of match did the Dudley Boys and D-Generation X compete at *Judgment Day 2000*?
   a. Ladder
   b. Texas Tornado
   c. Two-Out-of-Three Falls
   d. Double Tables

6. Who was the special guest referee for the sixty-minute Iron Man match for the WWE Championship at *Judgment Day 2000*?
   a. Shawn Michaels
   b. Chris Jericho
   c. Undertaker
   d. Kane

7. Who teamed with Edge & Christian to face Too Cool & Rikishi at *Judgment Day 2000*?
   a. Chris Jericho
   b. Gangrel
   c. Kurt Angle
   d. Matt Hardy

8. In what type of match did Kane and Triple H compete for the Intercontinental Championship at *Judgment Day 2001*?
   a. Inferno
   b. Chain
   c. Street Fight
   d. Casket

9. Who interfered in the No Holds Barred match for the WWE Championship, allowing Steve Austin to defeat Undertaker and retain the WWE Championship?
   a. Mr. McMahon
   b. The Rock
   c. Big Show
   d. Triple H

10. Who teamed with X-Pac for the Tag Team Turmoil match at *Judgment Day 2001?*
    a. K-Kwik
    b. Road Dogg
    c. Justin Credible
    d. Albert

JUDGMENT DAY 2002–2003

1. Who won the WWE Undisputed Championship at *Judgment Day 2002?*
    a. Undertaker
    b. Triple H
    c. Hulk Hogan
    d. The Rock

2. Who got the pinfall when Brock Lesnar and Paul Heyman met the Hardy Boys at *Judgment Day 2002?*
    a. Brock Lesnar
    b. Paul Heyman
    c. Matt Hardy
    d. Jeff Hardy

3. Who won the WWE Tag Team Championship at *Judgment Day 2002?*
    a. Billy & Chuck
    b. Dudley Boys
    c. Rikishi & Rico
    d. Test & William Regal

4. Who teamed to face Steve Austin in a Handicap match at *Judgment Day 2002?*
    a. Kane & Mankind
    b. Eddie Guerrero & Chavo Guerrero
    c. Kevin Nash & Scott Hall
    d. Ric Flair & Big Show

5. Who challenged Trish Stratus for the Women's Championship at *Judgment Day 2002*?
   - a. Stacy Keibler
   - b. Torrie Wilson
   - c. Jacqueline
   - d. Jazz

6. Who won the Battle Royal for the reinstated Intercontinental Championship at *Judgment Day 2003*?
   - a. Booker T
   - b. Christian
   - c. Test
   - d. Goldust

7. Who won the Fatal Four Way match for the WWE Women's Championship at *Judgment Day 2003*?
   - a. Victoria
   - b. Jacqueline
   - c. Jazz
   - d. Trish Stratus

8. Who hosted the Bikini Contest between Torrie Wilson and Sable at *Judgment Day 2003*?
   - a. Val Venis
   - b. Michael Cole
   - c. Tazz
   - d. Bradshaw

9. In what type of match did Brock Lesnar and Big Show compete at *Judgment Day 2003*?
   - a. Street Fight
   - b. Stretcher
   - c. First Blood
   - d. Biker Chain

10. What was the result of the Heavyweight Championship match between Triple H and Kevin Nash at *Judgment Day 2003*?
    a. Triple H won by pinfall.
    b. Triple H won by disqualification.
    c. Nash won by disqualification.
    d. Nash won by countout.

JUDGMENT DAY 2004–2005

1. Who teamed with Hardcore Holly to challenge Charlie Haas & Rico for the WWE Tag Team Championship at *Judgment Day 2004*?
   a. Funaki
   b. Billy Gunn
   c. Tajiri
   d. Matt Hardy

2. Whom did Chavo Guerrero defeat to win the Cruiserweight Championship at *Judgment Day 2004*?
   a. Jacqueline
   b. Miss Jackie
   c. Dawn Marie
   d. Victoria

3. Who challenged John Cena for the United States Championship at *Judgment Day 2004*?
   a. Mordecai
   b. Booker T
   c. Rene Dupree
   d. Mark Jindrak

4. What was the result of the WWE Championship match between Eddie Guerrero and JBL at *Judgment Day 2004*?
   a. Eddie Guerrero won by disqualification.
   b. JBL won by disqualification.
   c. JBL won by countout.
   d. The match was declared no contest.

5. Who teamed with Rob Van Dam to face the Dudley Boys at *Judgment Day 2004*?
   a. Tommy Dreamer   c. Rey Mysterio
   b. Spike Dudley   d. Jeff Hardy

6. Who teamed with Hardcore Holly to challenge MNM for the WWE Tag Team Championship at *Judgment Day 2005*?
   a. Nunzio   c. Shelton Benjamin
   b. Charlie Haas   d. Billy Gunn

7. Who successfully defended the United States Championship at *Judgment Day 2005*?
   a. Orlando Jordan   c. Booker T
   b. Carlito   d. Kurt Angle

8. In what type of match did John Cena and JBL compete for the WWE Championship at *Judgment Day 2005*?
   a. Barbed-Wire Steel Cage   c. Last Man Standing
   b. Falls Count Anywhere   d. "I Quit"

9. Who successfully defended the Cruiserweight
   Championship at *Judgment Day 2005*?
   a. Chavo Guerrero   c. Jamie Noble
   b. Paul London   d. Brian Kendrick

10. What was the result of the Eddie Guerrero vs. Rey Mysterio
    match at *Judgment Day 2005*?
    a. Eddie Guerrero won by disqualification.
    b. Rey Mysterio won by disqualification.
    c. Both men were disqualified.
    d. Both men were counted out.

JUDGMENT DAY 2006–2007

1. Who made his WWE Pay-Per-View debut at *Judgment Day
   2006*, pinning Undertaker?
   a. Mr. Kennedy   c. Great Khali
   b. Boogeyman   d. Umaga

2. Who was fired from *SmackDown!* by general manager
   Theodore Long at *Judgment Day 2006*?
   a. Finlay   c. Johnny Nitro
   b. Hardcore Holly   d. Simon Dean

3. Who challenged Gregory Helms for the Cruiserweight
   Championship at *Judgment Day 2006*?
   a. Matt Hardy   c. Psicosis
   b. Super Crazy   d. Sabu

4. What was the result of the World Heavyweight Championship match between Rey Mysterio and JBL at *Judgment Day 2006*?
   a. Rey Mysterio won by disqualification.
   b. JBL won by disqualification.
   c. Rey Mysterio pinned JBL.
   d. JBL pinned Rey Mysterio.

5. What Diva defeated Melina at *Judgment Day 2006*?
   a. Jillian Hall   c. Michelle McCool
   b. Victoria   d. Trish Stratus

6. Whom did Bobby Lashley pin to win his Handicap match at *Judgment Day 2007*?
   a. Vince McMahon   c. Umaga
   b. Shane McMahon   d. Test

7. How did Randy Orton win his match against Shawn Michaels at *Judgment Day 2007*?
   a. Orton won by pinfall.
   b. Orton won by submission.
   c. The referee stopped the match.
   d. Orton won by disqualification.

8. What was the result of the match that saw the Hardys successfully defend the World Team Championships against Lance Cade & Trevor Murdoch at *Judgment Day 2007*?
   a. Matt Hardy pinned Lance Cade.
   b. Jeff Hardy pinned Lance Cade.
   c. Matt Hardy pinned Trevor Murdoch.
   d. Jeff Hardy pinned Trevor Murdoch.

9. Who won the United States Championship at *Judgment Day 2007*?
   a. CM Punk
   b. Kane
   c. MVP
   d. William Regal

10. What was the result of the WWE Championship match between John Cena and Great Khali at *Judgment Day 2007*?
    a. Cena pinned Great Khali.
    b. Cena won by disqualification.
    c. Great Khali won by disqualification.
    d. Cena made Great Khali submit.

SECTION VII
ONE NIGHT STAND

ONE NIGHT STAND 2005–2006

1. Who did commentary with Joey Styles at the first ECW
   One Night Stand in 2005?
   - a. Rob Van Dam
   - b. Paul Heyman
   - c. Mick Foley
   - d. Tazz

2. The first *One Night Stand* featured a Three Way Dance.
   Who was *not* involved in the match?
   - a. Super Crazy
   - b. Tajiri
   - c. Little Guido
   - d. Spike Dudley

3. Who was the self-proclaimed leader of the anti-ECW group
   from *SmackDown!* that invaded ECW *One Night Stand*
   2005?
   - a. Kurt Angle
   - b. JBL
   - c. Edge
   - d. Big Show

4. Who teamed with Tommy Dreamer to face the Dudley
   Boys in the main event of ECW *One Night Stand 2005*?
   - a. Sabu
   - b. Rhyno
   - c. Raven
   - d. Sandman

5. What was the result of the match between Mike Awesome
   and Masato Tanaka at *One Night Stand 2005*?
   - a. Awesome pinned Tanaka.
   - b. Tanaka pinned Awesome.
   - c. Awesome made Tanaka submit.
   - d. Tanaka made Awesome submit.

6. Which individual did *not* appear in Lance Storm's corner or come to his aid in his match against Chris Jericho at *One Night Stand 2005*?

    a. Dawn Marie   c. Justin Credible
    b. Shane Douglas   d. Jason

7. How did the main event of ECW *One Night Stand 2005* end?

    a. Tommy Dreamer pinned Bubba Ray Dudley after hitting him with a barbed-wire baseball bat.
    b. The Dudley Boys pinned Tommy Dreamer after putting him through a flaming table.
    c. The Dudley Boys pinned Tommy Dreamer after throwing him off the balcony of the Hammerstein Ballroom.
    d. The match was declared no contest when the entire ECW locker room came out for a massive brawl in and out of the ring.

8. Whom did Steve Austin stun at the end of ECW *One Night Stand 2005* in a show of support for ECW?

    a. Shane McMahon   c. Vince McMahon
    b. Eric Bischoff   d. John Cena

9. Who faced Masato Tanaka in an Extreme Rules match at *One Night Stand 2006*?

    a. Mike Knox   c. Tracey Smothers
    b. Balls Mahoney   d. Big Show

10. What longtime ECW female teamed with Tommy
    Dreamer & Terry Funk in the Hardcore Inter-Gender
    match at *One Night Stand 2006*?
    a. Francine   c. Kimona Wanalaya
    b. Beulah   d. Dawn Marie

ONE NIGHT STAND 2006–2007

1. What was the result of the World Heavyweight
   Championship match between Rey Mysterio and Sabu at
   No Way Out 2006?
   a. Mysterio pinned Sabu.
   b. Sabu pinned Mysterio.
   c. Both men were disqualified.
   d. The match was declared no contest.

2. Who interfered in the main event match between John
   Cena and Rob Van Dam at *One Night Stand 2006*, helping
   Rob Van Dam win the WWE Championship?
   a. Sabu   c. Edge
   b. Big Show   d. Triple H

3. What was the result of the match between Kurt Angle and
   Randy Orton at *One Night Stand 2006*?
   a. Angle made Orton submit.
   b. Orton pinned Angle.
   c. Angle pinned Orton.
   d. Orton made Angle submit.

4. In what type of match did Candice Michelle and Melina compete at *One Night Stand 2007*?
   a. Jello
   b. Whipped Cream
   c. Pudding
   d. Mud

5. In what type of match did Mark Henry and Kane compete at *One Night Stand 2007*?
   a. Inferno
   b. Weapons
   c. Casket
   d. Lumberjack

6. Who challenged the Hardys for the World Tag Team Championship in a Ladder match at *One Night Stand 2007*?
   a. Paul London & Brian Kendrick
   b. World's Greatest Tag Team
   c. Highlanders
   d. Lance Cade & Trevor Murdoch

7. Who was *not* on the New Breed team that faced CM Punk & the ECW Originals at *One Night Stand 2007*?
   a. Kevin Thorn
   b. Elijah Burke
   c. Marcus Cor Von
   d. Matt Striker

8. What Florida city played host to *One Night Stand 2007*?
   a. Tampa
   b. Orlando
   c. Jacksonville
   d. Miami

9. Who defeated Randy Orton in a Stretcher match at *One Night Stand 2007*?
   a. Shawn Michaels
   b. Rob Van Dam
   c. Triple H
   d. Ric Flair

10. In what type of match did John Cena and Great Khali compete at *One Night Stand 2007*?
    a. Falls Count Anywhere
    b. Submission
    c. Punjabi Prison
    d. First Blood

SECTION VIII
VENGEANCE

VENGEANCE 2001–2002

1. Who was the guest referee when Matt Hardy met Jeff
   Hardy at *Vengeance 2001?*
   - a. Lita
   - b. Mick Foley
   - c. Edge
   - d. Michael Hayes

2. What Diva accompanied the Dudley Boys to the ring for
   their WWE World Tag Team Championship match at
   Vengeance 2001?
   - a. Trish Stratus
   - b. Terri Runnels
   - c. Ivory
   - d. Stacy Keibler

3. What Superstar teamed with Scotty 2 Hotty to face
   Christian and Test at *Vengeance 2001?*
   - a. Rikishi
   - b. Albert
   - c. Grandmaster Sexay
   - d. Spike Dudley

4. Who interfered in the Title Unification match at *Vengeance
   2001*, allowing Chris Jericho to become the Undisputed
   Champion?
   - a. Triple H
   - b. Booker T
   - c. The Rock
   - d. Kane

5. Which man in the Undisputed Championship tournament
   entered *Vengeance 2001* as WWE Champion?
   - a. Kurt Angle
   - b. Steve Austin
   - c. Chris Jericho
   - d. The Rock

6. What two members of the Un-Americans challenged Hulk Hogan & Edge for the WWE World Tag Team Championship at *Vengeance 2002*?
   a. Test & Christian
   b. Lance Storm & Test
   c. William Regal & Test
   d. Lance Storm & Christian

7. Who challenged Rob Van Dam for the Intercontinental Championship at *Vengeance 2002*?
   a. Eddie Guerrero
   b. Matt Hardy
   c. Brock Lesnar
   d. Kane

8. Who lost the WWE Championship at *Vengeance 2002* in a Triple-Threat match, despite not being pinned?
   a. Undertaker
   b. The Rock
   c. Kurt Angle
   d. Steve Austin

9. In what type of match did Booker T and Big Show compete at *Vengeance 2002*?
   a. Steel Cage
   b. No Disqualification
   c. Falls Count Anywhere
   d. Street Fight

10. Who challenged Jamie Noble for the Cruiserweight Championship match at *Vengeance 2002*?
    a. Tajiri
    b. Billy Kidman
    c. Scotty 2 Hotty
    d. Funaki

VENGEANCE 2003–2004

1. Who won the APA Invitational Bar Room Brawl at
   Vengeance 2003?
   a. Faarooq
   b. Bradshaw
   c. Brooklyn Brawler
   d. Matt Hardy

2. Vince McMahon faced Zach Gowen at *Vengeance 2003*.
   What is unique about Zach Gowen?
   a. He's legally blind.
   b. He's deaf.
   c. He has only one hand.
   d. He has only one leg.

3. What Superstar interfered, allowing Sable to defeat
   Stephanie McMahon at *Vengeance 2003?*
   a. A-Train
   b. Bull Buchanan
   c. John Cena
   d. Brock Lesnar

4. What Diva did Jamie Noble win a night with because of his
   victory over Billy Gunn at *Vengeance 2003?*
   a. Nidia
   b. Torrie Wilson
   c. Stacy Keibler
   d. Trish Stratus

5. At *Vengeance 2003*, who won the tournament for the vacant
   United States Championship?
   a. Rhyno
   b. Eddie Guerrero
   c. John Cena
   d. Rey Mysterio

6. What unique team challenged La Resistance for the World Tag Team Championship at *Vengeance 2004?*
   a. Cena & Edge
   b. Triple H & Eugene
   c. Ric Flair & Eugene
   d. Shawn Michaels & Shane McMahon

7. Who won a match to become the number one contender for the WWE Women's Championship at *Vengeance 2004?*
   a. Lita
   b. Ivory
   c. Molly Holly
   d. Victoria

8. Lance Cade teamed up with what WWE personality to face Tajiri & Rhyno at *Vengeance 2004?*
   a. Michael Cole
   b. Jonathan Coachman
   c. Eric Bischoff
   d. Paul Heyman

9. Who entered *Vengeance 2004* as the WWE Intercontinental Champion?
   a. Randy Orton
   b. Rob Van Dam
   c. Chris Jericho
   d. Christian

10. Who defeated Kane in a No Disqualification match at *Vengeance 2004?*
    a. Jeff Hardy
    b. Matt Hardy
    c. Tyson Tomko
    d. Val Venis

VENGEANCE 2005–2006

1. Whom did Lillian Garcia propose to at *Vengeance 2005*?
   - a. Val Venis
   - b. Viscera
   - c. Charlie Haas
   - d. Carlito

2. Victoria faced what *Playboy* cover girl at *Vengeance 2005*?
   - a. Torrie Wilson
   - b. Candice Michelle
   - c. Sable
   - d. Christy Hemme

3. Whom did John Cena pin in a Triple-Threat match to retain the WWE Championship at *Vengeance 2005*?
   - a. Christian
   - b. Jericho
   - c. Randy Orton
   - d. Chris Masters

4. Who tried to help Edge in his match against Kane at *Vengeance 2005*?
   - a. Matt Hardy
   - b. Snitsky
   - c. Hurricane
   - d. Christian

5. In what type of match did Triple H and Batista meet at *Vengeance 2005*?
   - a. Steel Cage
   - b. Street Fight
   - c. Three Stages of Hell
   - d. Hell in a Cell

6. What was the final result of the Two-Out-of-Three Falls match between Mick Foley and Ric Flair at *Vengeance 2006*?

   a. Flair won 2–1.   c. Flair won 2–0.
   b. Foley won 2–1.   d. Foley won 2–0.

7. Who won the Intercontinental Championship at *Vengeance 2006*?

   a. Shelton Benjamin   c. Randy Orton
   b. Carlito   d. Johnny Nitro

8. In what type of match did John Cena and Sabu compete at *Vengeance 2006*?

   a. Extreme Rules   c. Extreme Lumberjack
   b. Table   d. Ultimate Submission

9. Whom did D-Generation X face at *Vengeance 2006*?

   a. Rated RKO
   b. Highlanders & World's Greatest Tag Team
   c. Spirit Squad
   d. Mr. McMahon & Shane McMahon

10. Who faced an impostor version of himself at *Vengeance 2006*?

   a. Undertaker   c. Boogeyman
   b. Kane   d. Doink the Clown

VENGEANCE 2007

1. What Diva won the Women's Championship at *Vengeance 2007*?
   a. Mickie James
   b. Victoria
   c. Candice Michelle
   d. Melina

2. Whom did Cena pin in the WWE Championship Challenge to retain his title at *Vengeance 2007*?
   a. King Booker
   b. Mick Foley
   c. Bobby Lashley
   d. Randy Orton

3. Who teamed with Jimmy Snuka to challenge for the WWE Tag Team Championship at *Vengeance 2007*?
   a. Dusty Rhodes
   b. Kamala
   c. Sgt. Slaughter
   d. Arn Anderson

4. Who challenged MVP for the United States Championship at *Vengeance 2007*?
   a. Matt Hardy
   b. Carlito
   c. Super Crazy
   d. Ric Flair

5. Who won the vacant ECW Championship at *Vengeance 2007*?
   a. Tommy Dreamer
   b. CM Punk
   c. Johnny Nitro
   d. Elijah Burke

6. Who left *Vengeance 2007* as WWE Intercontinental Champion?
   a. Santino Marella
   b. Shelton Benjamin
   c. Umaga
   d. Jeff Hardy

7. How did Edge defeat Batista to retain the World Heavyweight Championship at *Vengeance 2007*?
   a. Edge pinned Batista.
   b. Edge made Batista submit.
   c. Batista was disqualified.
   d. Batista was counted out.

8. Who left *Vengeance 2007* as World Tag Team Champions?
   a. London & Kendrick
   b. Hardy Boys
   c. Cade & Murdoch
   d. Highlanders

9. What city played host to *Vengeance 2007*?
   a. New Orleans
   b. Phoenix
   c. Houston
   d. St. Louis

10. Who entered *Vengeance 2007* as WWE Cruiserweight Champion?
    a. Jamie Noble
    b. Chavo Guerrero
    c. Jimmy Wang Yang
    d. Hornswoggle

SECTION IX
GREAT AMERICAN BASH

GREAT AMERICAN BASH
2004–2005

1. Who was the first man gone from the Fatal Four Way Elimination match for the WWE United States Championship at *Great American Bash 2004*?
   a. John Cena
   c. Rene Dupree
   b. Rob Van Dam
   d. Booker T

2. What tag team faced Undertaker in a Concrete Crypt Handicap match at *Great American Bash 2004*?
   a. Dudley Boys
   b. Charlie Haas & Rico
   c. Hardcore Holly & Billy Gunn
   d. Kurt Angle & Luther Reigns

3. Who was the WWE Cruiserweight Champion heading in to *Great American Bash 2004*?
   a. Chavo Guerrero
   c. Rey Mysterio
   b. Spike Dudley
   d. Jamie Noble

4. In what type of match did Eddie Guerrero and JBL compete at *Great American Bash 2004*?
   a. Lumberjack
   c. Chain
   b. Texas Bullrope
   d. Street Fight

5. Who defeated Torrie Wilson at *Great American Bash 2004*?
   a. Miss Jackie
   c. Sable
   b. Nidia
   d. Victoria

6. Who was the United States Champion going in to *Great American Bash 2005*?
   a. Christian
   b. Orlando Jordan
   c. Booker T
   d. Paul London

7. Who was the special guest referee for the Bra and Panties match between Melina and Torrie Wilson at *Great American Bash 2005*?
   a. Jerry Lawler
   b. Val Venis
   c. Candice Michelle
   d. Maria

8. What member of the Mexicools got the pin when they defeated the bWo at *Great American Bash 2005*?
   a. Super Crazy
   b. Psicosis
   c. Juventud Guerrero
   d. Funaki

9. Whom did Undertaker defeat at *Great American Bash 2005* to become the number one contender for the World Heavyweight Championship?
   a. Mark Henry
   b. Eddie Guerrero
   c. Muhammad Hassan
   d. Rey Mysterio

10. What was the result of the World Heavyweight Championship match between Batista and JBL at *Great American Bash 2005*?
    a. JBL was disqualified.
    b. Batista pinned JBL.
    c. Both men were counted out.
    d. Batista was disqualified.

GREAT AMERICAN BASH 2006–2007

1. Who won the Fatal Four Way Bra and Panties match at *Great American Bash 2006*?
   - a. Kristal
   - b. Jillian
   - c. Ashley
   - d. Michelle McCool

2. Who challenged Finlay for the United States Championship at *Great American Bash 2006*?
   - a. Matt Hardy
   - b. Bobby Lashley
   - c. William Regal
   - d. Chavo Guerrero

3. Who faced Undertaker in the first-ever Punjabi Prison match at *Great American Bash 2006*?
   - a. Great Khali
   - b. Daivari
   - c. Mark Henry
   - d. Big Show

4. What team challenged Paul London & Brian Kendrick for the WWE Tag Team Championship at *Great American Bash 2006*?
   - a. Gymini
   - b. Pit Bulls
   - c. MNM
   - d. Mexicools

5. How did the match between Batista and Mr. Kennedy at
    Great American Bash 2006 end?
    a. Mr. Kennedy was disqualified.
    b. A time-limit draw.
    c. Batista was disqualified.
    d. Batista was counted out.

6. Who won the WWE Cruiserweight Championship at *Great
    American Bash 2007?*
    a. Shannon Moore   c. Jimmy Wang Yang
    b. Hornswoggle   d. Jamie Noble

7. In what type of match did Carlito and the Sandman
    compete at *Great American Bash 2007?*
    a. Extreme Rules   c. Falls Count Anywhere
    b. Summer Brawl   d. Singapore Cane on a Pole

8. Who challenged John Cena for the WWE Championship at
    Great American Bash 2007?
    a. Bobby Lashley   c. King Booker
    b. Mick Foley   d. Umaga

9. What legend did Randy Orton face in a Texas Bullrope
    match at *Great American Bash 2007?*
    a. Roddy Piper   c. Dusty Rhodes
    b. Jimmy Snuka   d. Ted DiBiase

10. Who left *Great American Bash 2007* as the World
    Heavyweight Champion?
    a. Batista   c. Great Khali
    b. Edge   d. Kane

SECTION X
SUPER STIPULATIONS

UNIQUE MATCHES

1. What 2006 Pay-Per-View saw the first-ever Punjabi Prison match?
   - a. *Judgment Day*
   - b. *Great American Bash*
   - c. *SummerSlam*
   - d. *Armageddon*

2. Whom did Mankind face in the first Boiler Room Brawl?
   - a. Kane
   - b. Big Boss Man
   - c. Undertaker
   - d. Triple H

3. Who lost his job as the result of losing a Pink Slip on a Pole match during the McMahon–Hemsley era on *Raw*?
   - a. The Rock
   - b. Steve Austin
   - c. British Bulldog
   - d. Mankind

4. Who faced Ken Shamrock in a Lion's Den match at *SummerSlam 1998*?
   - a. Dan Severn
   - b. Owen Hart
   - c. Al Snow
   - d. Steve Blackman

5. Who pinned Pat Patterson during his Evening Gown match with Gerald Brisco at *King of the Ring 2000* in order to win the WWE Hardcore Championship?
   - a. Raven
   - b. Hardcore Holly
   - c. Tommy Dreamer
   - d. Crash Holly

6. What odd character competed in the APA Invitational Bar Room Brawl at *Vengeance 2003*?
   a. Santa Claus
   c. Uncle Sam
   b. Easter Bunny
   d. Tooth Fairy

7. What Pay-Per-View saw the first Tables, Ladders & Chairs match in 2000?
   a. *Royal Rumble*
   c. *SummerSlam*
   b. *WrestleMania*
   d. *Survivor Series*

8. A spin of the wheel determined the type of match between Cactus Jack and Vader at *Halloween Havoc 1993*. Where did the wheel stop?
   a. First Blood
   c. Texas Death
   b. Falls Count Anywhere
   d. Barbed Wire

9. What was *not* one of the Three Stages of Hell when Shawn Michaels and Triple H wrestled for the World Heavyweight Championship at *Armageddon 2002*?
   a. Ladder
   c. Street Fight
   b. Submission
   d. Steel Cage

10. The Rock and Mankind wrestled for the WWE Championship in an empty arena at halftime of what Super Bowl?
    a. XXXI
    c. XXXIII
    b. XXXII
    d. XXXIV

ELIMINATION CHAMBER

1. At which 2002 event did the first Elimination Chamber event take place?
   a. *SummerSlam*
   b. *Great American Bash*
   c. *Survivor Series*
   d. *Armageddon*

2. Who was the last man to enter the match in the first Elimination Chamber match?
   a. Shawn Michaels
   b. Triple H
   c. Chris Jericho
   d. Rob Van Dam

3. Which two men scored two eliminations in the first Elimination Chamber match?
   a. Shawn Michaels and Triple H
   b. Booker T and Triple H
   c. Shawn Michaels and Chris Jericho
   d. Kane and Booker T

4. Who eliminated the most men at the Elimination Chamber match held at *New Year's Revolution 2005*?
   a. Randy Orton
   b. Triple H
   c. Edge
   d. Batista

5. Who eliminated Rob Van Dam from the Extreme Elimination Chamber match for the ECW World Championship at ECW *December to Dismember 2006*?
   a. Big Show
   b. Test
   c. Bobby Lashley
   d. CM Punk

6. Which was *not* an official weapon used in the Extreme Elimination Chamber match at ECW *December to Dismember 2006*?

   a. crowbar c. table

   b. stop sign d. barbed-wire baseball bat

7. Who was eliminated first from the Elimination Chamber match for the WWE Championship at *New Year's Revolution 2006*?

   a. Carlito c. Kane

   b. Chris Masters d. Kurt Angle

8. Who recorded multiple eliminations in the Elimination Chamber match at *New Year's Revolution 2006*?

   a. Shawn Michaels c. Carlito

   b. John Cena d. Kane

9. Who eliminated three Superstars from the Elimination Chamber match for the World Heavyweight Championship at *SummerSlam 2003*?

   a. Goldberg c. Randy Orton

   b. Triple H d. Shawn Michaels

10. Who was the first Superstar eliminated from the Elimination Chamber match at *SummerSlam 2003*?

    a. Chris Jericho c. Randy Orton

    b. Kevin Nash d. Shawn Michaels

HELL IN A CELL

1. Who faced Undertaker in the first Hell in a Cell to be featured at *WrestleMania*?
    a. Kevin Nash
    b. Big Boss Man
    c. Kane
    d. Big Show

2. Who won the first six-man Hell in a Cell, held at *Armageddon 2000*?
    a. Triple H
    b. The Rock
    c. Steve Austin
    d. Kurt Angle

3. Which Pay-Per-View featured the first Hell in a Cell match?
    a. *No Way Out*
    b. *Badd Blood*
    c. *Armageddon*
    d. *Great American Bash*

4. Who was the first Superstar to defend the WWE Championship in a Hell in a Cell match?
    a. Undertaker
    b. Triple H
    c. Shawn Michaels
    d. The Rock

5. Who first defeated Triple H in a one-on-one Hell in a Cell match?
    a. Chris Jericho
    b. Kevin Nash
    c. Shawn Michaels
    d. Batista

6. Who scored the pinfall in the D-Generation X vs.
    McMahons Handicap Hell in a Cell match at
    Unforgiven 2006?
    a. Triple H pinned Mr. McMahon.
    b. Shawn Michaels pinned Mr. McMahon.
    c. Triple H pinned Shane McMahon.
    d. Shawn Michaels pinned Shane McMahon.

7. Whom did Undertaker face in a Hell in a Cell match at
    Armageddon 2005?
    a. Mark Henry   c. Randy Orton
    b. Mr. Kennedy   d. Kane

8. Who was the special guest referee for the Kevin
    Nash–Triple H Hell in a Cell match at *Bad Blood
    2003*?
    a. Shawn Michaels   c. Undertaker
    b. Mick Foley   d. Ric Flair

9. In which Hell in a Cell matchup was a barbed-wire chair
    used for the first time?
    a. Triple H vs. Cactus Jack
    b. Triple H vs. Batista
    c. Triple H vs. Shawn Michaels
    d. Triple H vs. Kevin Nash

10. Who defended the WWE Championship against
    Undertaker in a Hell in a Cell match at *Great American
    Bash 2002*?

    a. Big Show   c. Triple H
    b. Kurt Angle   d. Brock Lesnar

SECTION XI
SUMMERSLAM

THE FIRST *SUMMERSLAM*

1. Who won the Intercontinental Championship at the initial *SummerSlam*?
   a. Bret Hart
   b. Texas Tornado
   c. Ultimate Warrior
   d. Ricky Steamboat

2. Who was the special guest referee when the Mega Powers and the Mega Bucks met in the main event of *SummerSlam 1988*?
   a. Sugar Ray Leonard
   b. Jesse Ventura
   c. Bobby Heenan
   d. Gorilla Monsoon

3. Who interfered in the Rick Rude–Junkyard Dog match, causing a disqualification?
   a. Honky Tonk Man
   b. Andre the Giant
   c. Big Boss Man
   d. Jake Roberts

4. Who was the guest on the *Brother Love Show* that was part of the first *SummerSlam*?
   a. Roddy Piper
   b. Tito Santana
   c. Mr. Perfect
   d. Jim Duggan

5. Whom did Bad News Brown defeat at the initial *SummerSlam*?
   a. Ken Patera
   b. Don Muraco
   c. Paul Orndorff
   d. Koko B. Ware

6. In what city was the first *SummerSlam* held?
   a. Boston
   b. Philadelphia
   c. New York
   d. Baltimore

7. Who managed the Powers of Pain for their match at *SummerSlam 1988*?
   a. Slick
   b. Mr. Fuji
   c. Bobby Heenan
   d. Baron

8. Whom did Jake Roberts face at the initial *SummerSlam*?
   a. Greg Valentine
   b. Hercules Hernandez
   c. Earthquake
   d. Bob Orton

9. How did the opening match at the first *SummerSlam* between the British Bulldogs and the Fabulous Rougeau Brothers end?
   a. Bulldogs won.
   b. Rougeaus won.
   c. A time-limit draw.
   d. Both teams were counted out.

10. Who defeated Koko B. Ware at *SummerSlam 1988*?
    a. Akeem
    b. Kamala
    c. Big Boss Man
    d. Warlord

SUMMERSLAM 1989–1990

1. Who teamed with the Rockers to face Rick Martel & the Fabulous Rougeau Brothers at *SummerSlam 1989*?
   a. Koko B. Ware
   b. Tito Santana
   c. Jimmy Snuka
   d. Dusty Rhodes

2. Who won the Intercontinental Championship at *SummerSlam 1989*?
   a. Mr. Perfect
   b. Ultimate Warrior
   c. Rick Rude
   d. Texas Tornado

3. What was the result of the *SummerSlam 1989* match featuring Demolition & Jim Duggan vs. Twin Towers & Andre the Giant?
   a. Andre the Giant pinned Duggan.
   b. Smash pinned Akeem.
   c. Big Boss Man pinned Ax.
   d. Andre the Giant pinned Smash.

4. Who teamed with Randy Savage to face Hulk Hogan & Brutus Beefcake at *SummerSlam 1989*?
   a. Ted DiBiase
   b. Earthquake
   c. Warlord
   d. Zeus

5. What was the result of the tag team match between the Hart Foundation and the Brain Busters at *SummerSlam 1989*?
   a. Tully Blanchard pinned Jim Neidhart.
   b. Bret Hart pinned Tully Blanchard.
   c. Arn Anderson pinned Bret Hart.
   d. Jim Neidhart pinned Arn Anderson.

6. In what type of match did the Ultimate Warrior defend the WWE Championship at *SummerSlam 1990*?
   a. Submission   c. No Disqualification
   b. Steel Cage   d. Falls Count Anywhere

7. How did Sensational Sherri win her match against Sapphire at *SummerSlam 1990*?
   a. pinfall   c. forfeit
   b. disqualification   d. submission

8. What was the final score of the Two-Out-of-Three Falls match for the World Tag Team Championship at *SummerSlam 1990*?
   a. Demolition won 2–0.
   b. Demolition won 2–1.
   c. Hart Foundation won 2–0.
   d. Hart Foundation won 2–1.

9. Who was the special guest referee for the match between Jake Roberts and Bad News Brown at *SummerSlam 1990*?
   a. Roddy Piper   c. Dusty Rhodes
   b. Big Boss Man   d. Rick Martel

10. Who was in Hulk Hogan's corner for his match against Earthquake at *SummerSlam 1990*?

    a. Tugboat   c. Big Boss Man

    b. Jim Duggan   d. Brutus Beefcake

SUMMERSLAM 1991–1992

1. Who was the Intercontinental Champion entering *SummerSlam 1991*?

    a. Mr. Perfect   c. Bret Hart

    b. Shawn Michaels   d. Rick Martel

2. Who was the guest referee for the Handicap match that featured Hulk Hogan & Ultimate Warrior facing Sgt. Slaughter, Col. Mustafa & General Adnan at *SummerSlam 1991*?

    a. Jesse Ventura   c. Randy Savage

    b. Sid Justice   d. Jim Duggan

3. In what type of match did Big Boss Man and the Mountie compete at *SummerSlam 1991*?

    a. Hard Time   c. Jail House

    b. Canadian Justice   d. Nightstick on a Pole

4. Which championship did *not* change hands at
   SummerSlam 1991?
   a. Intercontinental
   b. WWE
   c. WWE World Tag Team
   d. Million Dollar

5. Who accompanied the Bushwackers to the ring for their
   match against the Natural Disasters at *SummerSlam 1991*?
   a. Jimmy Snuka   c. George Steele
   b. Andre the Giant   d. British Bulldog

6. Who faced WWE Champion Randy Savage at *SummerSlam
   1992*?
   a. Ric Flair   c. Ultimate Warrior
   b. Mr. Perfect   d. Ted DiBiase

7. What was the result of the match between Shawn Michaels
   and Rick Martel at *SummerSlam 1992*?
   a. Michaels pinned Martel.
   b. Martel pinned Michaels.
   c. Both men were counted out.
   d. Both men were disqualified.

8. What boxing legend accompanied the British Bulldog to
   the ring for his Intercontinental Championship match
   against Bret Hart at *SummerSlam 1992*?
   a. George Foreman   c. Buster Douglas
   b. Lennox Lewis   d. Mike Tyson

9. What manager guided the Beverly Brothers when they challenged the Natural Disasters for the WWE World Tag Team Championship at *SummerSlam 1992*?
    a. Coach
    b. Harvey Wippleman
    c. Genius
    d. Jimmy Hart

10. Whom did Undertaker face at *SummerSlam 1992*?
    a. Jake Roberts
    b. Kamala
    c. Papa Shango
    d. Crush

SUMMERSLAM 1993–1994

1. Who teamed with the Smokin' Gunns to face Bam Bam Bigelow & the Headshrinkers at *SummerSlam 1993*?
    a. Owen Hart
    b. Tatanka
    c. Jim Duggan
    d. British Bulldog

2. What was the result of the WWE Championship match between Yokozuna and Lex Luger at *SummerSlam 1993*?
    a. Yokozuna pinned Luger.
    b. Luger won by countout.
    c. Luger won by disqualification.
    d. Yokozuna won by disqualification.

3. Whom did the Steiner Brothers defeat to win the WWE World Tag Team Championship at *SummerSlam 1993*?
    a. Nasty Boys
    b. Money Inc.
    c. Heavenly Bodies
    d. Well Dunn

4. How did Shawn Michaels win his Intercontinental Championship defense against Mr. Perfect at *SummerSlam 1993*?
   a. disqualification
   b. pinfall
   c. submission
   d. countout

5. In what type of match did Undertaker and Giant Gonzales compete at *SummerSlam 1993*?
   a. Casket
   b. Steel Cage
   c. Rest in Peace
   d. Buried Alive

6. Whom did Razor Ramon defeat at *SummerSlam 1994* to win the Intercontinental Championship?
   a. Jeff Jarrett
   b. 1-2-3 Kid
   c. Shawn Michaels
   d. Diesel

7. Who defeated Lex Luger at *SummerSlam 1994*, joining Ted DiBiase's Million Dollar Corporation?
   a. Bam Bam Bigelow
   b. Tatanka
   c. King Kong Bundy
   d. Adam Bomb

8. Who challenged Alundra Blayze for the WWE Women's Championship at *SummerSlam 1994*?
   a. Luna Vachon
   b. Sensational Sherri
   c. Bull Nakano
   d. Debbie Combs

9. Who led the fake Undertaker to the ring for his match against the real Undertaker at *SummerSlam 1994*?
   a. Brother Love
   b. Ted DiBiase
   c. Jimmy Hart
   d. Bobby Heenan

10. Who attacked Bret Hart after his match against Owen Hart at *SummerSlam 1994*?

a. Mr. Perfect

b. British Bulldog

c. Jim Neidhart

d. Jerry Lawler

SUMMERSLAM 1995–1996

1. What was the result of the match between Bret Hart and Isaac Yankem at *SummerSlam 1995*?

a. Hart pinned Yankem.

b. Yankem pinned Hart.

c. Hart won by countout.

d. Hart won by disqualification.

2. Whom did Undertaker face in a Casket match at *SummerSlam 1995*?

a. Adam Bomb

b. Kama

c. Sycho Sid

d. Savio Vega

3. Triple H made his *SummerSlam* debut in 1995 by defeating whom?

a. 1-2-3 Kid

b. Hardcore Holly

c. Goldust

d. Shane Douglas

4. Whom did Shawn Michaels defeat in a Ladder match at *SummerSlam 1995*?

a. Jeff Jarrett

b. Razor Ramon

c. Bob Backlund

d. Hakushi

5. What longtime manager accompanied Bertha Faye to the ring for her WWE Women's Championship victory over Alundra Blayze at *SummerSlam 1995*?
   a. Harvey Wippleman
   b. Sensational Sherri
   c. Paul Bearer
   d. Jimmy Hart

6. What tag team won the Fatal Four Way Elimination match for the WWE Tag Team Championship at *SummerSlam 1996*?
   a. Smokin' Gunns
   b. Bodydonnas
   c. New Rockers
   d. Godwinns

7. Future WWE Champion Steve Austin defeated what former WWE Champion in the Free-For-All match before *SummerSlam 1996*?
   a. Bob Backlund
   b. Ric Flair
   c. Sgt. Slaughter
   d. Yokozuna

8. Who saved Jake Roberts from further attacks by Jerry Lawler after he defeated Roberts at *SummerSlam 1996*?
   a. Mark Henry
   b. Bradshaw
   c. British Bulldog
   d. Ahmed Johnson

9. How did Owen Hart win his match against Savio Vega at *SummerSlam 1996*?
   a. submission
   b. pinfall
   c. TKO
   d. disqualification

10. Who challenged Shawn Michaels for the WWE
     Championship at *SummerSlam 1996*?
     a. Vader   c. Sycho Sid
     b. Bam Bam Bigelow   d. Undertaker

SUMMERSLAM 1997–1998

1. Who was the special guest referee for the WWE
    Championship match between Bret Hart and Undertaker
    at *SummerSlam 1997*?
    a. Roddy Piper   c. Jim Neidhart
    b. Shawn Michaels   d. Mr. McMahon

2. What did Bret Hart promise to do if he lost his match
    against Undertaker at *SummerSlam 1997*?
    a. retire
    b. burn a Canadian flag
    c. never wrestle in the United States again
    d. never wrestle for the WWE Championship again

3. Who defeated Brian Pillman at *SummerSlam 1997*,
    meaning Pillman had to wear a dress on the next
    night's *Raw*?
    a. Patriot   c. Vader
    b. Road Warrior Animal   d. Goldust

4. In what type of match did Mankind and Triple H compete at *SummerSlam 1997*?
   - a. Steel Cage
   - b. Boiler Room Brawl
   - c. Falls Count Anywhere
   - d. "I Quit"

5. Who challenged British Bulldog for the European Championship at *SummerSlam 1997*?
   - a. D'Lo Brown
   - b. Jeff Jarrett
   - c. Ken Shamrock
   - d. Al Snow

6. What member of the Oddities pinned all four members of Kaientai at *SummerSlam 1998*?
   - a. Golga
   - b. Kurggan
   - c. Giant Silva
   - d. Luna Vachon

7. What was the result of the WWE Championship match pitting Steve Austin against Undertaker at *SummerSlam 1998*?
   - a. Austin pinned Undertaker.
   - b. Both men were disqualified.
   - c. Austin won by disqualification.
   - d. The match was declared no contest.

8. Who teamed with Sable to face Marc Mero & Jacqueline in a Mixed Tag Team match at *SummerSlam 1998*?
   - a. Matt Hardy
   - b. Edge
   - c. Val Venis
   - d. Ken Shamrock

9. In what type of match did X-Pac and Jeff Jarrett compete at *SummerSlam 1998*?
   a. Southern Justice
   b. Hair vs. Hair
   c. Steel Cage
   d. Two-Out-of-Three Falls

10. The New Age Outlaws faced Mankind in a Handicap match for the WWE Tag Team Championship at *SummerSlam 1998*. Who was supposed to be Mankind's partner?
   a. Triple H
   b. The Rock
   c. Kane
   d. Shawn Michaels

SUMMERSLAM 1999

1. What weapon did Ken Shamrock use on Steve Blackman to win their Lion's Den Weapons match at *SummerSlam 1999*?
   a. steel chair
   b. nunchuks
   c. kendo stick
   d. baseball bat

2. Who defeated the Big Boss Man at *SummerSlam 1999*, winning the WWE Hardcore Championship?
   a. Al Snow
   b. Raven
   c. Road Dogg
   d. Mark Henry

3. Who won the tag team Turmoil match at *SummerSlam 1999*?
   a. Edge & Christian
   b. Acolytes
   c. Mideon & Viscera
   d. New Brood

4. Who successfully defended the WWE Women's Championship at *SummerSlam 1999*?
   a. Tori
   b. Lita
   c. Ivory
   d. Jacqueline

5. Who helped Jeff Jarrett beat D'Lo Brown at *SummerSlam 1999*, winning both the Intercontinental and European championships?
   a. Road Dogg
   b. Godfather
   c. Mark Henry
   d. Howard Finkel

6. Who was the special guest referee for the Triple Threat match for the WWE Championship at *SummerSlam 1999*?
   a. Sgt. Slaughter
   b. Jesse Ventura
   c. Mr. McMahon
   d. Jerry Lawler

7. What was the result of the WWE Tag Team Championship match at *SummerSlam 1999* pitting Big Show & Undertaker against X-Pac & Kane?
   a. X-Pac pinned Big Show.
   b. Undertaker pinned X-Pac.
   c. Kane pinned Undertaker.
   d. Big Show pinned Kane.

8. How did Test win his Love Her or Leave Her Greenwich Street Fight against Shane McMahon at *SummerSlam 1999*?
   a. Test pinned Shane.
   b. Test made Shane submit.
   c. Stephanie McMahon threw in the towel for her brother.
   d. Test won by TKO.

9. In what type of match did The Rock and Mr. Ass compete at *SummerSlam 1999*?
   a. Kiss My Ass
   b. "I Quit"
   c. Brahma Bull Strap
   d. *SmackDown!* Hotel

10. Who won the WWE Championship at *SummerSlam 1999*?
    a. Steve Austin
    b. Triple H
    c. Undertaker
    d. Mankind

SUMMERSLAM 2000–2001

1. Who won the Intercontinental Championship in a tag team match at *SummerSlam 2000*?
   a. Val Venis
   b. Chyna
   c. Eddie Guerrero
   d. Trish Stratus

2. In what type of match did the Kat and Terri compete at *SummerSlam 2000*?
   a. Bra and Panties
   b. Evening Gown
   c. Stinkface
   d. Strap

3. Who successfully defended the WWE Championship at *SummerSlam 2000?*
   a. The Rock
   b. Triple H
   c. Undertaker
   d. Kurt Angle

4. Who challenged Shane McMahon for his WWE Hardcore Championship at *SummerSlam 2000?*
   a. Al Snow
   b. Kane
   c. Steve Blackman
   d. Mick Foley

5. What member of the Right to Censor scored the pinfall when they defeated Too Cool & Rikishi at *SummerSlam 2000?*
   a. Steven Richards
   b. Ivory
   c. Bull Buchanan
   d. Goodfather

6. Who defeated Lance Storm for the Intercontinental Championship at *SummerSlam 2001?*
   a. William Regal
   b. Rhyno
   c. Chris Jericho
   d. Edge

7. In what type of match did the Brothers of Destruction face Diamond Dallas Page & Kanyon at *SummerSlam 2001?*
   a. Last Ride
   b. Texas Tornado
   c. Steel Cage
   d. No Disqualification

8. Who won the WCW Championship at *SummerSlam 2001?*
   a. The Rock
   b. Booker T
   c. Chris Jericho
   d. Kurt Angle

9. Who teamed with the APA to face the Dudley Boys & Test at *SummerSlam 2001*?

    a. Al Snow   c. Spike Dudley

    b. Tazz   d. Tommy Dreamer

10. Who won a Ladder match for the WWE Hardcore Championship at *SummerSlam 2001*?

    a. Jeff Hardy   c. Rob Van Dam

    b. Matt Hardy   d. Billy Gunn

SUMMERSLAM 2002–2003

1. Who won the WWE Championship at *SummerSlam 2002*?

    a. Kurt Angle   c. Steve Austin

    b. The Rock   d. Brock Lesnar

2. Who faced Undertaker at *SummerSlam 2002*?

    a. Test   c. Tazz

    b. Steven Richards   d. Hulk Hogan

3. Who won the Intercontinental Championship at *SummerSlam 2002*?

    a. Eddie Guerrero   c. Rob Van Dam

    b. Ric Flair   d. Chris Jericho

4. In what type of match did Triple H and Shawn Michaels compete at *SummerSlam 2002?*
   - a. Three Stages of Hell
   - b. Hell in a Cell
   - c. Last Man Standing
   - d. Unsanctioned Street Fight

5. What team successfully defended the WWE Tag Team Championship at *SummerSlam 2002?*
   - a. Hulk Hogan & Edge
   - b. Un-Americans
   - c. Dudley Boys
   - d. Booker T & Goldust

6. Who won the Fatal Four Way match for the United States Championship at *SummerSlam 2003?*
   - a. Rhyno
   - b. Tajiri
   - c. Eddie Guerrero
   - d. Chris Benoit

7. Who successfully defended the WWE Championship at *SummerSlam 2003?*
   - a. Randy Orton
   - b. Kurt Angle
   - c. Big Show
   - d. Brock Lesnar

8. In what type of match did Kane and Rob Van Dam compete at *SummerSlam 2003?*
   - a. Inferno
   - b. Ladder
   - c. No Holds Barred
   - d. Ambulance

9. Who faced Eric Bischoff in a No Disqualification Falls Count Anywhere match at *SummerSlam 2003?*
   - a. Steve Austin
   - b. Shane McMahon
   - c. Mr. McMahon
   - d. Stephanie McMahon

10. What Diva accompanied A-Train to the ring for his match against Undertaker at *SummerSlam 2003*?
   a. Trish Stratus
   b. Sable
   c. Torrie Wilson
   d. Nidia

SUMMERSLAM 2004–2005

1. What was the result of the WWE Championship match between JBL and Undertaker at *SummerSlam 2004*?
   a. JBL won by disqualification.
   b. Undertaker won by disqualification.
   c. JBL pinned Undertaker.
   d. Both men were counted out.

2. Who was *not* involved in the Triple-Threat match for the Intercontinental Championship at *SummerSlam 2004*?
   a. Chris Jericho
   b. Batista
   c. Edge
   d. Christian

3. Who faced Matt Hardy in a Till Death Do Us Part match at *SummerSlam 2004*?
   a. Snitsky
   b. Kane
   c. Ric Flair
   d. Test

4. In what type of match did the Divas compete at *SummerSlam 2004*?
   a. Dance Competition
   b. Diva Talent Competition
   c. Diva Dodgeball
   d. Diva Water Fight

5. Who won the World Heavyweight Championship at
   SummerSlam 2004?
   a. Randy Orton   c. Shawn Michaels
   b. Triple H   d. John Cena

6. What was the result of the Legend vs. Icon match at
   SummerSlam 2005 pitting Hulk Hogan against Shawn
   Michaels?
   a. Michaels pinned Hogan.
   b. Hogan pinned Michaels.
   c. Both men were counted out.
   d. Hogan won by disqualification.

7. Who accompanied Eugene to the ring for his match
   against Kurt Angle at *SummerSlam 2005?*
   a. Trish Stratus   c. Christy Hemme
   b. Stacy Keibler   d. Torrie Wilson

8. In what type of match did Rey Mysterio and Eddie
   Guerrero compete at *SummerSlam 2005?*
   a. Steel Cage   c. Ladder
   b. Last Man Standing d. Falls Count Anywhere

9. Who challenged John Cena for the WWE Championship at
   SummerSlam 2005?
   a. Triple H   c. Chris Jericho
   b. Edge   d. Christian

10. Who challenged Batista for the World Heavyweight
    Championship at *SummerSlam 2005*?
    a. Randy Orton   c. JBL
    b. Undertaker   d. Booker T

SUMMERSLAM 2006–2007

1. In what type of match did Ric Flair and Mick Foley
   compete at *SummerSlam 2006*?
   a. Hardcore   c. "I Quit"
   b. Submission   d. Steel Cage

2. Who did *not* interfere in the D-Generation X vs. Shane and
   Mr. McMahon match on behalf of the McMahons at
   SummerSlam 2006?
   a. William Regal   c. Mr. Kennedy
   b. Finlay   d. Carlito

3. What was the result of the WWE Championship match
   between Edge and John Cena at *SummerSlam 2006*?
   a. Cena pinned Edge.
   b. Edge pinned Cena.
   c. Edge won by disqualification.
   d. Cena won by disqualification.

4. What was the result of the World Heavyweight Championship match between King Booker and Batista at *SummerSlam 2006*?
   a. King Booker pinned Batista.
   b. Batista pinned King Booker.
   c. King Booker won by disqualification.
   d. Batista won by disqualification.

5. Who faced Hulk Hogan at *SummerSlam 2006*?
   a. Rey Mysterio   c. Randy Orton
   b. Big Show   d. Kurt Angle

6. Who won the Interpromotional Divas Battle Royal at *SummerSlam 2007*?
   a. Mickie James   c. Candice Michelle
   b. Michelle McCool   d. Beth Phoenix

7. Who was *not* involved in the Triple-Threat match for the Intercontinental Championship at *SummerSlam 2007*?
   a. Mr. Kennedy   c. Jeff Hardy
   b. Umaga   d. Carlito

8. In what type of contest were Matt Hardy and MVP supposed to compete at *SummerSlam 2007*?
   a. pizza eating   c. video game
   b. beer drinking   d. free-throw shooting

9. Who was the World Heavyweight Champion heading in to *SummerSlam 2007*?

    a. Great Khali   c. Batista

    b. Undertaker   d. Edge

10. Who successfully defended the ECW Championship at *SummerSlam 2007*?

    a. CM Punk   c. Tommy Dreamer

    b. Big Daddy V   d. John Morrison

SECTION XII
UNFORGIVEN

UNFORGIVEN 1998–1999

1. Who challenged Luna Vachon to an Evening Gown match at *Unforgiven 1998*?
   a. Sunny
   b. Kat
   c. Sable
   d. Terri Runnels

2. Who successfully defended the NWA World Tag Team Championship at *Unforgiven 1998*?
   a. Rock 'n' Roll Express
   b. Legion of Doom
   c. New Midnight Express
   d. Headbangers

3. What type of match did Kane and Undertaker compete in at *Unforgiven 1998*, the first time for WWE?
   a. Last Ride
   b. Boiler Room Brawl
   c. Inferno
   d. Buried Alive

4. Who challenged Steve Austin for the WWE Championship at *Unforgiven 1998*?
   a. The Rock
   b. Ken Shamrock
   c. Dude Love
   d. Mankind

5. For what championship did Triple H and Owen Hart compete at *Unforgiven 1998*?
   a. European
   b. Intercontinental
   c. Hardcore
   d. United States

6. Whom did Triple H pin when he won the WWE
    Championship in a Six-Pack Challenge at *Unforgiven 1999*?
    a. British Bulldog   c. Big Show
    b. The Rock   d. Kane

7. Who was the special outside enforcer for the Six-Pack
    Challenge, for the WWE Championship, at *Unforgiven
    1999*?
    a. Steve Austin   c. Ken Shamrock
    b. Undertaker   d. Mankind

8. Who faced the Big Boss Man in a Kennel From Hell match
    at *Unforgiven 1999*?
    a. X-Pac   c. Al Snow
    b. Christian   d. D'Lo Brown

9. Who was the scab referee for the opening match—Val
    Venis vs. Steve Blackman—at *Unforgiven 1999*?
    a. Roddy Piper   c. Brooklyn Brawler
    b. Sgt. Slaughter   d. Ricky Steamboat

10. Who challenged Jeff Jarrett for the Intercontinental
    Championship at *Unforgiven 1999*?
    a. Edge   c. Chyna
    b. Chris Jericho   d. Mark Henry

UNFORGIVEN 2000–2001

1. Who won the Hardcore Battle Royal for the WWE Hardcore Championship at *Unforgiven 2000*?
   a. Perry Saturn
   b. Al Snow
   c. Crash Holly
   d. Steve Blackman

2. In what type of match did Tazz and Jerry Lawler compete at *Unforgiven 2000*?
   a. Kiss My Foot
   b. Steel Cage
   c. Strap
   d. Philadelphia Street Fight

3. Who won the Fatal Four Way match for the WWE Championship at *Unforgiven 2000*?
   a. Chris Benoit
   b. Kane
   c. The Rock
   d. Undertaker

4. Who was the special guest referee when Triple H and Kurt Angle met in a No DQ match at *Unforgiven 2000*?
   a. Shane McMahon
   b. Mick Foley
   c. Steve Austin
   d. Stephanie McMahon

5. Who got the pin when the Right to Censor defeated the Dudley Boys and Acolytes at *Unforgiven 2000*?
   a. Val Venis
   b. Steven Richards
   c. Bull Buchanan
   d. Goodfather

6. Whom did Eddie Guerrero successfully defeat for the Intercontinental Championship at *Unforgiven 2000*?
   a. Billy Gunn   c. X-Pac
   b. Rikishi   d. Chris Jericho

7. What tag team won the Fatal Four Way Elimination match for the WWE Tag Team Championship at *Unforgiven 2001*?
   a. Hardy Boys
   b. Dudley Boys
   c. Big Show & Spike Dudley
   d. Lance Storm & Hurricane

8. Who challenged the Brothers of Destruction for the WCW Tag Team Championship at *Unforgiven 2001*?
   a. Ken Shamrock & Steve Blackman
   b. Diamond Dallas Page & Chuck Palumbo
   c. KroniK
   d. Perry Saturn & Raven

9. Who teamed with Shane McMahon to face The Rock in a Handicap match for the WCW Championship at *Unforgiven 2001*?
   a. Test   c. Chris Jericho
   b. Booker T   d. Rob Van Dam

10. Who won the WCW United States Championship at *Unforgiven 2001*?
    a. Tajiri   c. Rhyno
    b. William Regal   d. Tommy Dreamer

UNFORGIVEN 2002–2003

1. Who got the pin when the team of Kane, Goldust,
    Booker T, and Bubba Ray Dudley faced the Un-Americans
    at *Unforgiven 2002?*
    a. Kane   c. Booker T
    b. Goldust   d. Bubba Ray Dudley

2. What was the result of the WWE Championship match
    between Brock Lesnar and Undertaker at *Unforgiven 2002?*
    a. Lesnar pinner Undertaker.
    b. Undertaker won by disqualification.
    c. Lesnar won by disqualification.
    d. Both men were disqualified.

3. Whom did Trish Stratus successfully defeat for the
    Women's Championship at *Unforgiven 2002?*
    a. Torrie Wilson   c. Ivory
    b. Molly Holly   d. Jazz

4. Who challenged Triple H for the World Heavyweight
    Championship at *Unforgiven 2002?*
    a. Kane   c. Rob Van Dam
    b. Kurt Angle   d. Booker T

5. Who was the Intercontinental Champion heading in to
    Unforgiven 2002?
    a. Ric Flair   c. Chris Jericho
    b. Rey Mysterio   d. Christian

6. What was the result of the match between the teams of Jim Ross & Jerry Lawler and Al Snow & Jonathan Coachman at *Unforgiven 2003*?
   a. Lawler pinned Snow.
   b. Coach pinned J.R.
   c. J.R. pinned Coach.
   d. Snow pinned Lawler.

7. Who successfully defended the Intercontinental Championship in a Triple-Threat match at *Unforgiven 2003*?
   a. Rob Van Dam
   b. Christian
   c. Chris Jericho
   d. Edge

8. Who accompanied Test to the ring for his match against Scott Steiner at *Unforgiven 2003*?
   a. Sable
   b. Stacy Keibler
   c. Trish Stratus
   d. Torrie Wilson

9. What was the result of the Tag Team match between the teams of Trish Stratus & Lita and Molly Holly & Gail Kim at *Unforgiven 2003*?
   a. Trish Stratus pinned Gail Kim.
   b. Gail Kim pinned Lita.
   c. Lita pinned Molly Holly.
   d. Molly Holly pinned Trish Stratus.

10. Who left *Unforgiven 2003* as the World Heavyweight Champion?
    a. Triple H
    b. Shawn Michaels
    c. Goldberg
    d. Randy Orton

UNFORGIVEN 2004–2005

1. In what type of match did Shawn Michaels and Kane compete at *Unforgiven 2004*?
   a. Inferno
   b. Street Fight
   c. Lumberjack
   d. No Disqualification

2. Who won the Intercontinental Championship at *Unforgiven 2004*?
   a. Shelton Benjamin
   b. Chris Jericho
   c. Christian
   d. William Regal

3. Who did *not* interfere on Triple H's behalf during his World Heavyweight Championship match against Randy Orton at *Unforgiven 2004*?
   a. Jonathan Coachman
   b. Ric Flair
   c. Mr. McMahon
   d. Batista

4. Who accompanied Trish Stratus to the ring for her WWE Women's Championship match against Victoria at *Unforgiven 2004*?
   a. Viscera
   b. Tyson Tomko
   c. Test
   d. Albert

5. Who successfully defended the World Tag Team Championship at *Unforgiven 2004*?
   a. Tajiri & Rhyno
   b. Booker T & Goldust
   c. La Resistance
   d. Dudley Boys

6. What was the result of the WWE Championship match between John Cena and Kurt Angle at *Unforgiven 2005*?
   a. Cena won by pinfall.
   b. Angle won by disqualification.
   c. Both men were counted out.
   d. Both men were disqualified.

7. What Diva got the pin when the teams of Trish Status & Ashley and Victoria & Torrie Wilson met at *Unforgiven 2005*?
   a. Trish Stratus
   b. Ashley
   c. Victoria
   d. Torrie Wilson

8. In what type of match did Matt Hardy and Edge compete at *Unforgiven 2005*?
   a. TLC
   b. Last Man Standing
   c. Steel Cage
   d. "I Quit"

9. Who won the Intercontinental Championship at *Unforgiven 2005*?
   a. Carlito
   b. Shelton Benjamin
   c. Rob Van Dam
   d. Ric Flair

10. Kerwin White wrestled at *Unforgiven 2005*. What other name is Kerwin White known by?
    a. Gene Snitsky
    b. Tajiri
    c. Chavo Guerrero
    d. Chuck Palumbo

UNFORGIVEN 2006–2007

1. Who would have had to leave *Raw* if he'd lost his match at *Unforgiven 2006*?
   - a. Kane
   - b. Randy Orton
   - c. Johnny Nitro
   - d. John Cena

2. What was the result of the match between Kane and Umaga at *Unforgiven 2006*?
   - a. Umaga pinned Kane.
   - b. Kane pinned Umaga.
   - c. Both men were counted out.
   - d. Kane won by disqualification.

3. Whom did Trish Stratus face in her retirement match at *Unforgiven 2006*?
   - a. Mickie James
   - b. Victoria
   - c. Lita
   - d. Melina

4. Who successfully defended the World Tag Team Championship at *Unforgiven 2006*?
   - a. Lance Cade & Trevor Murdoch
   - b. Highlanders
   - c. Cryme Tyme
   - d. Spirit Squad

5. Who challenged Johnny Nitro for the Intercontinental Championship at *Unforgiven 2006*?
   a. Carlito
   b. Super Crazy
   c. Jeff Hardy
   d. Jim Duggan

6. What was the result of the WWE Championship match at *Unforgiven 2007*?
   a. John Cena won by disqualification.
   b. Randy Orton won by disqualification.
   c. Both men were counted out.
   d. Both men were disqualified.

7. Whom did Undertaker defeat in his return to WWE at *Unforgiven 2007*?
   a. Finlay
   b. Mark Henry
   c. Kane
   d. Mr. Kennedy

8. Who challenged Candice Michelle for the WWE Women's Championship at *Unforgiven 2007*?
   a. Beth Phoenix
   b. Mickie James
   c. Jillian Hall
   d. Michelle McCool

9. What was the unique stipulation of the Triple H vs. Carlito match at *Unforgiven 2007*?
   a. Both men were blindfolded.
   b. Carlito could not be disqualified.
   c. Triple H had one hand tied behind his back.
   d. Carlito was chained to Shawn Michaels.

10. What was the result of the match between MVP & Matt Hardy and Deuce & Domino at *Unforgiven 2007*?

    a. MVP pinned Deuce.
    b. MVP pinned Domino.
    c. Matt Hardy pinned Deuce.
    d. Matt Hardy pinned Domino.

SECTION XIII
FORMER EVENTS

IN YOUR HOUSE

1. What Superstar made his debut at the first *In Your House*, saving Razor Ramon from a double team at the hands of Jeff Jarrett and the Roadie?
   a. Diesel
   b. Savio Vega
   c. Aldo Montoya
   d. Triple H

2. Where was the first *In Your House* held?
   a. Fort Wayne, IN
   b. Kansas City, MO
   c. Syracuse, NY
   d. Hartford, CT

3. Who was the WWE Champion heading in to the first *In Your House*?
   a. Shawn Michaels
   b. Bret Hart
   c. Diesel
   d. Undertaker

4. Who won the Intercontinental Championship at the second *In Your House: The Lumberjacks*?
   a. British Bulldog
   b. Shawn Michaels
   c. Jeff Jarrett
   d. Razor Ramon

5. Who attacked British Bulldog during his championship match at *In Your House: Great White North*, allowing Diesel to retain the title?
   a. Owen Hart
   b. Sycho Sid
   c. Triple H
   d. Bret Hart

6. Whom did Bret Hart defeat inside a steel cage, retaining the WWE Championship at *In Your House: Rage in the Cage*?

    a. Shawn Michaels

    b. Vader

    c. Undertaker

    d. Diesel

7. Whom did Undertaker defeat in the first Buried Alive match at *In Your House: Buried Alive*?

    a. Vader

    b. Executioner

    c. Crush

    d. Mankind

8. What member of the Hart Foundation got the pin when their team defeated Steve Austin, Ken Shamrock, Goldust, and the Legion of Doom at *In Your House: Canadian Stampede*?

    a. Bret Hart

    b. British Bulldog

    c. Jim Neidhart

    d. Owen Hart

9. Who won a Fatal Four Way match for the WWE Tag Team Championship at *In Your House: Ground Zero*?

    a. Headbangers

    b. Legion of Doom

    c. Godwinns

    d. Owen Hart & British Bulldog

10. Who debuted at *In Your House: St. Valentine's Day Massacre*, helping Mr. McMahon in his Steel Cage match against Steve Austin?

    a. Chris Jericho

    b. Tiger Ali Singh

    c. Big Show

    d. Rakishi

NEW YEAR'S REVOLUTION

1. Who challenged Shelton Benjamin to a rematch right after he lost the first match for the Intercontinental Championship at *New Year's Revolution 2005*?
   a. Hurricane
   b. Maven
   c. Rob Conway
   d. Heidenreich

2. Who defeated Jerry Lawler at *New Year's Revolution 2005*?
   a. Eugene
   b. Snitsky
   c. Zach Gowen
   d. Muhammad Hassan

3. Who was the special guest referee for the Elimination Chamber match at *New Year's Revolution 2005*?
   a. Kevin Nash
   b. Shane McMahon
   c. Shawn Michaels
   d. Ric Flair

4. Who won the Bra and Panties Gauntlet match at *New Year's Revolution 2006*?
   a. Maria
   b. Candice Michelle
   c. Ashley
   d. Torrie Wilson

5. Who wrestled for two different championships at *New Year's Revolution 2006*?
   a. Ric Flair
   b. Shawn Michaels
   c. Edge
   d. Triple H

6. Whom did Shelton Benjamin defeat, with the aid of Momma Benjamin, at *New Year's Revolution 2006*?

   a. Hardcore Holly

   b. Viscera

   c. Charlie Haas

   d. Bobby Lashley

7. In what type of match did Johnny Nitro and Jeff Hardy compete for the Intercontinental Championship at *New Year's Revolution 2007*?

   a. Ladder

   b. Street Fight

   c. Falls Count Anywhere

   d. Steel Cage

8. What team won the Tag Team Turmoil match at *New Year's Revolution 2007*?

   a. Cryme Tyme

   b. Highlanders

   c. Cade & Murdoch

   d. World's Greatest Tag Team

9. What was the result of the match between Rated RKO and D-Generation X at *New Year's Revolution 2007*?

   a. D-Generation X won by pinfall.

   b. Rated RKO won by pinfall.

   c. D-Generation X won by disqualification.

   d. The match was declared no contest.

10. Who challenged Mickie James for the Women's Championship at *New Year's Revolution 2007*?

    a. Melina

    b. Victoria

    c. Candice Michelle

    d. Beth Phoenix

KING OF THE RING 1987–1993

1. Whom did Randy Savage defeat in the finals to win *King of the Ring 1987*?
    a. Junkyard Dog
    b. Rick Martel
    c. Jake Roberts
    d. King Kong Bundy

2. Who won *King of the Ring 1989*?
    a. Rick Martel
    b. Tito Santana
    c. Jimmy Snuka
    d. Haku

3. Who won *King of the Ring 1991*?
    a. Sid Justice
    b. Bret Hart
    c. Shawn Michaels
    d. Undertaker

4. What city played host to every *King of the Ring* tournament from 1987 through 1991?
    a. Providence
    b. Boston
    c. New York
    d. Philadelphia

5. Who won the WWE Championship at *King of the Ring 1993*?
    a. Undertaker
    b. Randy Savage
    c. Yokozuna
    d. Hulk Hogan

6. What *King of the Ring 1993* tournament quarterfinalist had to wrestle three first-round matches against the same opponent because the first two ended in time-limit draws?
   a. Lex Luger
   b. Mr. Perfect
   c. Bret Hart
   d. Razor Ramon

7. When the quartet of the Smokin' Gunns and the Steiner Brothers defeated the Headshrinkers and Money Inc. at *King of the Ring 1993*, who got the pinfall for the winning side?
   a. Billy Gunn
   b. Bart Gunn
   c. Rick Steiner
   d. Scott Steiner

8. Who challenged Shawn Michaels for the Intercontinental Championship at *King of the Ring 1993*?
   a. Owen Hart
   b. Diesel
   c. Papa Shango
   d. Crush

9. Who received a bye into the finals of *King of the Ring 1993* when Lex Luger and Tatanka battled to a draw in the quarterfinals?
   a. Mr. Perfect
   b. Bret Hart
   c. Bam Bam Bigelow
   d. Razor Ramon

10. Who won *King of the Ring 1993*?
    a. Mr. Perfect
    b. Bret Hart
    c. Bam Bam Bigelow
    d. Razor Ramon

KING OF THE RING 1994–1996

1. Who faced Jerry Lawler at *King of the Ring 1994*?
   - a. Tatanka
   - b. Jake Roberts
   - c. Roddy Piper
   - d. British Bulldog

2. Who helped Owen Hart win *King of the Ring 1994* by interfering in the final match?
   - a. Jeff Jarrett
   - b. Jim Neidhart
   - c. British Bulldog
   - d. Bret Hart

3. Who won *King of the Ring 1995*?
   - a. Shawn Michaels
   - b. Mabel
   - c. Owen Hart
   - d. Irwin R. Schyster

4. Who teamed with Diesel to face the duo of Sycho Sid & Tatanka at *King of the Ring 1995*?
   - a. Razor Ramon
   - b. Bam Bam Bigelow
   - c. Shawn Michaels
   - d. 1-2-3 Kid

5. What was the result of the Kiss My Foot match between Bret Hart and Jerry Lawler at *King of the Ring 1995*?
   - a. Lawler won by pinfall.
   - b. Lawler won by disqualification.
   - c. Hart won by pinfall.
   - d. Hart won by submission.

6. Who won the Intercontinental Championship at *King of the Ring 1996*?
   a. Razor Ramon
   b. Triple H
   c. Ahmed Johnson
   d. Bob Holly

7. Who was the special guest referee for the WWE Championship match between Shawn Michaels and the British Bulldog at *King of the Ring 1996*?
   a. Owen Hart
   b. Mr. Perfect
   c. Bret Hart
   d. Diesel

8. Whom did Steve Austin defeat in the semifinals to reach the finals of *King of the Ring 1996*?
   a. Triple H
   b. Marc Mero
   c. Yokozuna
   d. Ultimate Warrior

9. What duo challenged the Smokin' Gunns for the Tag Team Championship at *King of the Ring 1996*?
   a. Headbangers
   b. Bodydonnas
   c. Godwinns
   d. New Rockers

10. What was the result of the match between Undertaker and Mankind at *King of the Ring 1997*?
    a. Undertaker pinned Mankind.
    b. Mankind pinned Undertaker.
    c. Undertaker won by disqualification.
    d. Mankind won by TKO.

KING OF THE RING 1997–1998

1. Who challenged Undertaker for the WWE Championship
   at *King of the Ring 1997*?
   a. Goldust
   b. Faarooq
   c. Ahmed Johnson
   d. Ken Shamrock

2. What was the result of the match between Shawn Michaels
   and Steve Austin at *King of the Ring 1997*?
   a. Both men were counted out.
   b. Austin pinned Michaels.
   c. Michaels pinned Austin.
   d. Both men were disqualified.

3. Who teamed with the Legion of Doom to face the Hart
   Foundation team of Owen Hart, British Bulldog &
   Jim Neidhart at *King of the Ring 1997*?
   a. Vader
   b. Crush
   c. Sycho Sid
   d. Brian Pillman

4. Whom did Triple H defeat in the finals to win *King of the
   Ring 1997*?
   a. Jerry Lawler
   b. Mankind
   c. Savio Vega
   d. Flash Funk

5. *King of the Ring 1998* featured the famous Hell in a Cell between Undertaker and Mankind. In what city did that brutal bout take place?
   - a. Cleveland
   - b. Providence
   - c. Pittsburgh
   - d. Indianapolis

6. Who won *King of the Ring 1998*?
   - a. Mark Henry
   - b. Jeff Jarrett
   - c. Marc Mero
   - d. Ken Shamrock

7. Who was the special guest referee when Too Much faced Al Snow & Head at *King of the Ring 1998*?
   - a. Mankind
   - b. Big Boss Man
   - c. Jerry Lawler
   - d. Sable

8. Who teamed with "Bodacious" Bart Gunn as the New Midnight Express to challenge the New Age Outlaws for the Tag Team Championship at *King of the Ring 1998*?
   - a. "Sublime" Scorpio
   - b. "Bombastic" Bob Holly
   - c. "Vivacious" Vader
   - d. "Dapper" Dan Severn

9. Who won the WWE Championship at *King of the Ring 1998*?
   - a. The Rock
   - b. Triple H
   - c. Kane
   - d. Steve Austin

10. Who teamed with the Headbangers to face Kaientai at *King of the Ring 1998*?
    - a. X-Pac
    - b. Owen Hart
    - c. Taka Michinoku
    - d. Val Venis

KING OF THE RING 1999–2000

1. Who won *King of the Ring 1999*?
   a. Kurt Angle
   b. Mr. Ass
   c. X-Pac
   d. Road Dogg

2. Chyna qualified for the quarterfinals of *King of the Ring 1999* by defeating what Superstar in the first round?
   a. Jeff Jarrett
   b. Test
   c. Droz
   d. Val Venis

3. What did Mr. McMahon & Shane McMahon gain by defeating Steve Austin in a Ladder match at *King of the Ring 1999*?
   a. Austin couldn't challenge for the WWE Championship for one year.
   b. They won Austin's 50 percent share in WWE.
   c. Austin could not attack either man for the rest of the year unless physically provoked.
   d. Austin was suspended for three months.

4. What was the result of the WWE Championship match between Undertaker and The Rock at *King of the Ring 1999*?
   a. The Rock pinned Undertaker.
   b. The Rock won by disqualification.
   c. Undertaker pinned The Rock.
   d. Undertaker won by disqualification.

5. What was the result of the tag team match between the
   Hardys and Edge & Christian at *King of the Ring 1999*?
   a. Edge pinned Matt.   c. Christian pinned Jeff.
   b. Matt pinned Christian.   d. Jeff pinned Edge.

6. Who teamed with Kane & Undertaker to face Triple H,
   Mr. McMahon & Shane McMahon at *King of the Ring 2000*?
   a. Steve Austin   c. The Rock
   b. Mankind   d. Eddie Guerrero

7. In what type of match did D-Generation X & Tori and the
   Dudley Boys compete at *King of the Ring 2000*?
   a. Handicap TLC
   b. Handicap Elimination
   c. Handicap Tables Dumpster
   d. Handicap Baseball Bat on a Pole

8. Kurt Angle won three tournament matches at *King of the
   Ring 2000*. Whom did he *not* defeat on his way to claiming
   the title?
   a. Val Venis   c. Rikishi
   b. Chris Jericho   d. Crash Holly

9. What team won the Four Corners Elimination match for
   the World Tag Team Championship at *King of the
   Ring 2000*?
   a. Test & Albert   c. Edge & Christian
   b. Hardys   d. Too Cool

10. In what type of match did Gerald Briscoe and Pat Patterson compete at *King of the Ring 2002*?

    a. Evening Gown   c. Dumpster

    b. Pink Slip on a Pole   d. Jello

KING OF THE RING 2001–2002

1. Whom did Edge *not* defeat en route to winning *King of the Ring 2001*?

    a. Kurt Angle   c. Raven

    b. Perry Saturn   d. Rhyno

2. Kurt Angle wrestled three matches on *King of the Ring 2001*. Whom did he *not* wrestle?

    a. Edge   c. Rikishi

    b. Christian   d. Shane McMahon

3. Who attacked Steve Austin halfway through his Triple-Threat match against Chris Benoit and Chris Jericho at *King of the Ring 2001*?

    a. Booker T   c. Triple H

    b. Diamond Dallas Page d. Rob Van Dam

4. Who challenged Jeff Hardy for the WWE Light Heavyweight Championship at *King of the Ring 2001*?

    a. Scotty 2 Hotty   c. Dean Malenko

    b. X-Pac   d. Matt Hardy

5. What was the result of the WWE Championship match between the Dudley Boys and Spike Dudley & Kane at *King of the Ring 2001*?
    a. Kane pinned Bubba Ray.
    b. Bubba Ray pinned Spike.
    c. Spike pinned D'Von.
    d. D'Von pinned Kane.

6. Who interfered in the WWE Undisputed Championship match between Undertaker and Triple H at *King of the Ring 2002*?
    a. Kane   c. The Rock
    b. Ric Flair   d. Steve Austin

7. What was the result of the match between Hulk Hogan and Kurt Angle at *King of the Ring 2002*?
    a. Hogan pinned Angle.
    b. Angle made Hogan submit.
    c. Hogan won by disqualification.
    d. Angle pinned Hogan.

8. Whom did Brock Lesnar defeat in the finals to win *King of the Ring 2002*?
    a. Test   c. Kane
    b. Chris Jericho d. Rob Van Dam

9. Who won the WWE Cruiserweight Championship at *King of the Ring 2002*?
    a. Hurricane   c. Jamie Noble
    b. Spike Dudley   d. Tajiri

10. Who won the Women's Championship at *King of the Ring 2002?*

    a. Molly Holly   c. Lita

    b. Trish Stratus   d. Victoria

SECTION XIV
NO MERCY

NO MERCY 1999–2000

1. In what unique match did Chyna and Jeff Jarrett compete at *No Mercy 1999*?
   - a. Women's Place
   - b. Good Housekeeping
   - c. Maid in the Shade
   - d. Battle of the Sexes

2. Who won the Four Corners Elimination match at *No Mercy 1999*?
   - a. Kane
   - b. X-Pac
   - c. Faarooq
   - d. Bradshaw

3. Who won the WWE Women's Championship at *No Mercy 1999*?
   - a. Ivory
   - b. Sable
   - c. Tori
   - d. Fabulous Moolah

4. In what type of match did Edge & Christian and the New Brood compete at *No Mercy 1999*?
   - a. Texas Tornado Tag
   - b. Ladder
   - c. Steel Cage
   - d. First Blood

5. Who interfered in the WWE Championship match at *No Mercy 1999*, allowing Triple H to retain the championship?
   - a. Chyna
   - b. The Rock
   - c. Undertaker
   - d. Mankind

6. What tag team did the Dudley Boys eliminate last to win the Dudley Boys Invitational Tables match at *No Mercy 2000*?
   - a. Too Cool
   - b. Goodfather & Bull Buchanan
   - c. Lo Down
   - d. Tazz & Raven

7. In what type of match for the WWE Championship did Kurt Angle and The Rock compete at *No Mercy 2000*?
   - a. Submission
   - b. Hardcore
   - c. Iron Man
   - d. No Disqualification

8. Who faced Chris Jericho in a Steel Cage match at *No Mercy 2000*?
   - a. William Regal
   - b. Eddie Guerrero
   - c. X-Pac
   - d. Edge

9. What was the result of the No Holds Barred match between Steve Austin and Rikishi at *No Mercy 2000*?
   - a. Austin pinned Rikishi.
   - b. Rikishi pinned Austin.
   - c. The match was declared no contest.
   - d. Rikishi was counted out.

10. Who teamed with Chyna to face Val Venis & Steven Richards at *No Mercy 2000*?
    - a. Eddie Guerrero
    - b. Perry Saturn
    - c. Billy Gunn
    - d. Road Dogg

NO MERCY 2001–2002

1. Whom did Steve Austin pin in a Triple-Threat match to retain the WWE Championship at *No Mercy 2001*?
   - a. Booker T
   - b. Kurt Angle
   - c. Eddie Guerrero
   - d. Rob Van Dam

2. Whom did Edge defeat in a Ladder match at *No Mercy 2001* to win the Intercontinental Championship?
   - a. Test
   - b. William Regal
   - c. Christian
   - d. Billy Kidman

3. What unlikely duo challenged the Dudley Boys for the WWE World Tag Team Championship at *No Mercy 2001*?
   - a. Kane & Scotty 2 Hotty
   - b. Big Show & Tajiri
   - c. Lance Storm & Chyna
   - d. Diamond Dallas Page & Hurricane

4. In what type of match did Stacy Keibler and Torrie Wilson compete at *No Mercy 2001*?
   - a. Evening Gown
   - b. Pillow Fight
   - c. Lingerie
   - d. Bra and Panties

5. Who left *No Mercy 2001* as the WCW Champion?
   - a. The Rock
   - b. Chris Jericho
   - c. Undertaker
   - d. Triple H

6. Whom did Torrie Wilson defeat at *No Mercy 2002*?
   a. Lita
   b. Dawn Marie
   c. Gail Kim
   d. Jazz

7. Who defended the WWE Women's Championship at *No Mercy 2002*?
   a. Trish Stratus
   b. Mighty Molly
   c. Nidia
   d. Victoria

8. Who accompanied Brock Lesnar to the ring for his WWE Championship match against Undertaker at *No Mercy 2002*?
   a. Sable
   b. Kurt Angle
   c. Big Show
   d. Paul Heyman

9. Who successfully defended the WWE Cruiserweight Championship at *No Mercy 2002*?
   a. Rey Mysterio
   b. Tajiri
   c. Jamie Noble
   d. Spike Dudley

10. Who tried to interfere on behalf of Kane in the Title Unification match at *No Mercy 2002*?
    a. Hurricane
    b. Mankind
    c. Ric Flair
    d. Rob Van Dam

NO MERCY 2003–2004

1. Who threw in the towel for Stephanie McMahon, ending her "I Quit" match against Mr. McMahon at *No Mercy 2003*?
   a. Zach Gowen
   b. Triple H
   c. Linda McMahon
   d. Shane McMahon

2. Whom did Zach Gowen defeat at *No Mercy 2003*?
   a. Matt Hardy
   b. Shannon Moore
   c. A-Train
   d. Shane McMahon

3. Who accompanied the Basham Brothers to the ring for their match at *No Mercy 2003*?
   a. Mercedes
   b. Shantell
   c. Shaniqua
   d. Kimber

4. Who won the WWE United States Championship at *No Mercy 2003*?
   a. Eddie Guerrero
   b. Kurt Angle
   c. John Cena
   d. Big Show

5. In what type of match did Brock Lesnar and Undertaker compete for the WWE Championship at *No Mercy 2003*?
   a. Bike Chain
   b. Buried Alive
   c. Casket
   d. Ultimate Submission

6. Who won the United States Championship at *No Mercy 2004*?
   a. Eddie Guerrero
   b. Booker T
   c. John Cena
   d. Orlando Jordan

7. What was the result of the match pitting Rico, Charlie Haas & Miss Jackie vs. the Dudley Boys & Dawn Marie at *No Mercy 2004*?
   a. Dawn Marie pinned Miss Jackie.
   b. Miss Jackie pinned Dawn Marie.
   c. Rico pinned D-Von.
   d. Bubba Ray pinned Charlie Haas.

8. What duo retained the WWE Tag Team Championship at *No Mercy 2004*?
   a. Rey Mysterio & Rob Van Dam
   b. Nunzio & Johnny Stamboli
   c. Kenzo Suzuki & Rene Dupree
   d. Billy Kidman & Paul London

9. In what type of match did JBL and Undertaker compete for the WWE Championship at *No Mercy 2004*?
   a. Texas Bullrope
   b. Last Ride
   c. Stretcher
   d. No Disqualification

10. Who successfully defended the WWE Cruiserweight Championship at *No Mercy 2004*?
    a. Scotty 2 Hotty
    b. Spike Dudley
    c. Nunzio
    d. Tajiri

NO MERCY 2005–2007

1. Who challenged Batista for the World Heavyweight Championship at *No Mercy 2005*?
   a. Eddie Guerrero
   b. Orlando Jordan
   c. Booker T
   d. Christian

2. What was the result of the match at *No Mercy 2005* between the Legion of Doom & Christy Hemme and MNM?
   a. Melina pinned Christy Hemme.
   b. Christy Hemme pinned Melina.
   c. Johnny Nitro pinned Heidenreich.
   d. Animal pinned Joey Mercury.

3. Who won the WWE Cruiserweight Championship at *No Mercy 2005*?
   a. Nunzio
   b. Juventud
   c. Super Crazy
   d. Psicosis

4. Who attacked Hardcore Holly after his match against Mr. Kennedy at *No Mercy 2005*?
   a. Paul Birchill
   b. William Regal
   c. Sylvan
   d. Chavo Guerrero

5. What was the result of the Handicap Casket match between Undertaker and Randy Orton & "Cowboy" Bob Orton at *No Mercy 2005*?
   a. Undertaker put Bob Orton in the casket.
   b. Undertaker put Randy Orton in the casket.
   c. Undertaker put Randy & Bob Orton in the casket.
   d. Randy & Bob Orton put Undertaker in the casket.

6. Whom did King Booker pin in the Fatal Four Way World Heavyweight Championship match at *No Mercy 2006* to retain his championship?
   a. Batista
   b. Bobby Lashley
   c. Finlay
   d. William Regal

7. In what type of match did Rey Mysterio and Chavo Guerrero compete at *No Mercy 2006*?
   a. Steel Cage
   b. Falls Count Anywhere
   c. Ladder
   d. Street Fight

8. Who accompanied Paul London & Brian Kendrick to the ring for their WWE Tag Team Championship match at *No Mercy 2006*?
   a. Ashley
   b. Michelle McCool
   c. Torrie Wilson
   d. Kelly Kelly

9. Who was the WWE Champion when the dust settled at *No Mercy 2007*?
   a. Triple H
   b. Randy Orton
   c. John Cena
   d. Umaga

10. Who won the WWE Women's Championship at *No Mercy 2007*?

    a. Mickie James   c. Melina

    b. Beth Phoenix   d. Jillian Hall

SECTION XV

TABOO TUESDAY
CYBER SUNDAY

TABOO TUESDAY 2004-2005

1. Against whom did Chris Jericho defend the Intercontinental Championship at the first *Taboo Tuesday*
   in 2004?
   a. Christian   c. Batista
   b. Shelton Benjamin   d. William Regal

2. What type of match did fans choose for the Ric Flair–
   Randy Orton bout at *Taboo Tuesday 2004*?
   a. Submission   c. Strap
   b. Falls Count Anywhere d. Steel Cage

3. What did fans choose for the Weapon of Choice match
   between Snitsky and Kane at *Taboo Tuesday 2004*?
   a. steel chair   c. chain
   b. lead pipe   d. brass knuckles

4. Against whom did Triple H defend the World Heavyweight
   Championship at *Taboo Tuesday 2004*?
   a. Shawn Michaels   c. Kurt Angle
   b. Edge   d. John Cena

5. What city played host to the first *Taboo Tuesday*?
   a. Chicago   c. Detroit
   b. Minneapolis   d. Milwaukee

6. Who was the last Diva eliminated by Trish Stratus, when she retained the WWE Women's Championship, in a Fulfill Your Fantasy Battle Royal at *Taboo Tuesday 2004*?
   a. Nidia
   b. Molly Holly
   c. Victoria
   d. Gail Kim

7. Whom did Big Show & Kane defeat to win the World Tag Team Championship at *Taboo Tuesday 2005*?
   a. Cade & Murdoch
   b. Carlito & Masters
   c. Snitsky & Heidenreich
   d. Val Venis & Viscera

8. Who assisted Jonathan Coachman in his match against Batista at *Taboo Tuesday 2005*?
   a. Wild Samoans
   b. Paul Orndorff & Bob Orton
   c. Earthquake & Typhoon
   d. Vader & Goldust

9. What type of outfit did fans choose for the Fulfill Your Fantasy Battle Royal at *Taboo Tuesday 2005*?
   a. leather and lace
   b. nurses' uniforms
   c. lingerie
   d. cheerleading outfits

10. Against whom did Ric Flair defend the Intercontinental Championship at *Taboo Tuesday 2005*?
    a. Triple H
    b. Carlito
    c. Shelton Benjamin
    d. Chris Masters

CYBER SUNDAY 2006-2007

1. Whom did fans vote as the special guest referee when D-Generation X met Rated RKO at *Cyber Sunday 2006*?
   a. Jonathan Coachman   c. Vince McMahon
   b. Eric Bischoff   d. Shane McMahon

2. Who won the WWE Women's Championship at *Cyber Sunday 2006*?
   a. Lita   c. Melina
   b. Mickie James   d. Victoria

3. Who won the main event match at *Cyber Sunday 2006* that featured the WWE Champion, World Heavyweight Champion, and ECW Champion?
   a. John Cena   c. King Booker
   b. Bobby Lashley   d. Big Show

4. Who won the Texas Tornado match at *Cyber Sunday 2006*?
   a. Highlanders
   b. Cryme Tyme
   c. Charlie Haas & Viscera
   d. Lance Cade & Trevor Murdoch

5. Whom did the fans vote to challenge Jeff Hardy for the Intercontinental Championship at *Cyber Sunday 2006*?
   a. Johnny Nitro   c. Carlito
   b. Umaga   d. Shelton Benjamin

6. Who won the Halloween Costume Contest at *Cyber Sunday*
   2007?
   - a. Mickie James
   - b. Torrie Wilson
   - c. Kelly Kelly
   - d. Layla

7. Whom did the fans vote to challenge CM Punk for the
   ECW Championship at *Cyber Sunday 2007*?
   - a. Big Daddy V
   - b. Miz
   - c. John Morrison
   - d. Elijah Burke

8. Who faced MVP for the United States Championship at
   Cyber Sunday 2007?
   - a. Matt Hardy
   - b. Kane
   - c. Mark Henry
   - d. Great Khali

9. In what type of match did Triple H and Umaga compete at
   Cyber Sunday 2007?
   - a. First Blood
   - b. Steel Cage
   - c. Sledgehammer on a Pole
   - d. Street Fight

10. Whom did the fans vote special guest referee for the World
    Heavyweight Championship match between Batista and
    Undertaker at *Cyber Sunday 2007*?
    - a. Mick Foley
    - b. Steve Austin
    - c. JBL
    - d. Jerry Lawler

SECTION XVI
SURVIVOR SERIES

SURVIVOR SERIES 1987–1989

1. Who was the sole survivor when Hulk Hogan's team met Andre the Giant's team in the main event of *Survivor Series 1987*?
   - a. Hulk Hogan
   - b. Andre the Giant
   - c. Bam Bam Bigelow
   - d. Rick Rude

2. Who were the only survivors in the women's match at *Survivor Series 1987*?
   - a. Glamour Girls
   - b. Fabulous Moolah and Rockin' Robin
   - c. Sensational Sherri and Donna Christanello
   - d. Jumping Bomb Angels

3. Who was *not* a survivor when the team of Randy Savage, Ricky Steamboat, Jake Roberts, Jim Duggan, and Brutus Beefcake wrestled in the opening match at *Survivor Series 1987*?
   - a. Randy Savage
   - b. Ricky Steamboat
   - c. Jake Roberts
   - d. Brutus Beefcake

4. What Ohio city played host to *Survivor Series 1987* and *1988*?
   - a. Akron
   - b. Dayton
   - c. Columbus
   - d. Richfield

5. On what day of the week did *Survivor Series 1988* take place?

    a. Thursday   c. Saturday

    b. Friday   d. Sunday

6. What tag team was the only survivor from the Ten-on-Ten Tag Team Survivor match from *Survivor Series 1988*?

    a. Demolition   c. Rockers

    b. Powers of Pain   d. Hart Foundation

7. Who was the last man eliminated by Hulk Hogan's team during the main event of *Survivor Series 1988*?

    a. Ted DiBiase   c. Akeem

    b. Big Boss Man   d. Haku

8. Who was *not* a member of the *Hulkamaniacs* team that faced the Million Dollar Team at *Survivor Series 1989*?

    a. Demolition Ax   c. Jake Roberts

    b. Demolition Smash   d. Brutus Beefcake

9. Who was the sole survivor from the match featuring the Rude Brood and Roddy's Rowdies at *Survivor Series 1989*?

    a. Jimmy Snuka   c. Rick Rude

    b. Roddy Piper   d. Mr. Perfect

10. Who was the only member of Randy Savage's team *not* to survive when the King's Court met the 4 × 4's at *Survivor Series 1989*?

    a. Randy Savage   c. Dino Bravo

    b. Earthquake   d. Greg Valentine

SURVIVOR SERIES 1990–1991

1. Who was the only survivor when the Alliance—Nikolai Volkoff, Tito Santana & the Bushwackers—met the Mercenaries—Sgt. Slaughter, Boris Zhukov & the Orient Express—at *Survivor Series 1990*?
   a. Sgt. Slaughter
   b. Nikolai Volkoff
   c. Boris Zhukov
   d. Tito Santana

2. Who was *not* a member of the Ultimate Warrior's team that faced the Perfect Team at *Survivor Series 1990*?
   a. Hawk
   b. Animal
   c. Jim Duggan
   d. Texas Tornado

3. Who was the last member of the team eliminated by Hulk Hogan, Ultimate Warrior, and Tito Santana during the Grand Finale match at *Survivor Series 1990*?
   a. Ted DiBiase
   b. Rick Martel
   c. Hercules
   d. Warlord

4. Who was the captain of the team that featured a debuting Undertaker as its mystery member at *Survivor Series 1990*?
   a. Earthquake
   b. Mr. Perfect
   c. Ted DiBiase
   d. Rick Martel

5. What team managed to win its match at *Survivor Series 1990* without having a single member eliminated?
   a. Visionaries
   b. *Hulkamaniacs*
   c. Dream Team
   d. Vipers

6. Who was the only survivor when the team of Ric Flair, Mountie, Ted DiBiase & Warlord met the team of Roddy Piper, Bret Hart, Virgil & Davey Boy Smith at *Survivor Series 1991*?
   a. Bret Hart
   b. Roddy Piper
   c. Ric Flair
   d. Ted DiBiase

7. Who was the only member of the team featuring the Nasty Boys and the Beverly Brothers to be eliminated at *Survivor Series 1991*?
   a. Blake Beverly
   b. Beau Beverly
   c. Knobbs
   d. Sags

8. Who interfered in the championship match between Hulk Hogan and Undertaker at *Survivor Series 1991*, allowing Undertaker to become WWE Champion?
   a. Jake Roberts
   b. Ric Flair
   c. Randy Savage
   d. Earthquake

9. Who teamed with the Natural Disasters for their match against the Legion of Doom & Big Boss Man at *Survivor Series 1991*?
   a. Barbarian
   b. I.R.S.
   c. Hercules
   d. Skinner

10. What was the tagline for *Survivor Series 1991*?
    a. Dead Man Walking
    b. Hell on Earth
    c. Gravest Challenge
    d. The Death of *Hulkamania*?

SURVIVOR SERIES 1992-1993

1. When the Nasty Boys & Natural Disasters met the Beverly
    Brothers & Money Inc. at *Survivor Series 1992*, which tag
    team survived?
    a. Nasty Boys
    b. Natural Disasters
    c. Beverly Brothers
    d. Money Inc.

2. How did Bret Hart retain his championship against Shawn
    Michaels at *Survivor Series 1992*?
    a. Hart pinned Michaels.
    b. Hart made Michaels submit.
    c. Michaels was disqualified.
    d. Michaels was counted out.

3. Randy Savage was to team with Ultimate Warrior against
    Ric Flair and Razor Ramon at *Survivor Series 1992*. Who
    replaced the Ultimate Warrior?
    a. Diesel
    b. Jake Roberts
    c. Mr. Perfect
    d. Crush

4. What future WWE Champion made his debut at *Survivor
    Series 1992*, defeating Virgil?
    a. Lex Luger
    b. Yokozuna
    c. Sycho Sid
    d. Diesel

5. In what type of match did Big Boss Man and Nailz compete at *Survivor Series 1992*?

   a. Nightstick on a Pole   c. Prison Rules

   b. Lockdown   d. Hard Time

6. Who was the only member of the Hart Family eliminated in the match against Shawn Michaels and his knights at *Survivor Series 1993*?

   a. Bret Hart   c. Bruce Hart

   b. Owen Hart   d. Keith Hart

7. Which knight was not on Shawn Michaels's team for his match against the Hart Family at *Survivor Series 1993*?

   a. Black Knight   c. Red Knight

   b. White Knight   d. Blue Knight

8. Who was the only survivor when the All-Americans team—Lex Luger, Undertaker, and the Steiner Brothers—met the Foreign Fanatics—Yokozuna, Crush, Ludvig Borga, and Jacques Rougeau—at *Survivor Series 1993*?

   a. Undertaker   c. Yokozuna

   b. Lex Luger   d. Crush

9. What other federation's tag team championship was defended in a match between the Heavenly Bodies and the Rock 'n' Roll Express at *Survivor Series 1993*?

   a. ECW

   b. NWA

   c. Smokey Mountain Wrestling

   d. AWA

10. What two tag teams dressed as Doink for their Tag Team match at *Survivor Series 1993*?
    a. Headshrinkers & Bushwackers
    b. Bushwackers & Men on a Mission
    c. Smokin' Gunns & Men on a Mission
    d. Smokin' Gunns & Razor Ramon & the 1-2-3 Kid

SURVIVOR SERIES 1994–1996

1. Who was the special guest enforcer when Undertaker and Yokozuna met in a Casket match at *Survivor Series 1994*?
   a. Arnold Schwarzenegger   c. George Foreman
   b. Chuck Norris   d. Walter Payton

2. Who was the only survivor when Razor Ramon's Bad Guys met Shawn Michaels's Teamsters at *Survivor Series 1994*?
   a. Shawn Michaels   c. 1-2-3 Kid
   b. Diesel   d. Razor Ramon

3. Who was in Bret Hart's corner when he faced Bob Backlund for the WWE Championship at *Survivor Series 1994*?
   a. Stu Hart   c. Jim Neidhart
   b. Davey Boy Smith   d. Owen Hart

4. What was the name of the team featuring Lex Luger, Mabel, Adam Bomb, and the Smokin' Gunns at *Survivor Series 1994*?
   a. Stars-N-Stripes
   b. Guts 'n' Glory
   c. Allied Powers
   d. American Made

5. Who won the WWE Championship at *Survivor Series 1995*?
   a. Diesel
   b. Shawn Michaels
   c. Yokozuna
   d. Bret Hart

6. Who was the only survivor when the Bodydonnas met the Underdogs at *Survivor Series 1995*?
   a. 1-2-3 Kid
   b. Bob Holly
   c. Bodydonna Skip
   d. Marty Jannetty

7. Who was the only Superstar eliminated from the team of Shawn Michaels, Ahmed Johnson, Davey Boy Smith, and Sycho Sid that competed at *Survivor Series 1995*?
   a. Shawn Michaels
   b. Ahmed Johnson
   c. Davey Boy Smith
   d. Sycho Sid

8. Who won the WWE Championship at *Survivor Series 1996*?
   a. Sycho Sid
   b. Bret Hart
   c. Shawn Michaels
   d. Undertaker

9. Who survived when the team of Faarooq, Vader, Razor Ramon II, and Diesel II met Flash Funk, Jimmy Snuka, Savio Verga, and Yokozuna at *Survivor Series 1996*?
   a. Vader
   b. Yokozuna
   c. Faarooq and Diesel II
   d. No one survived

10. Who faced Undertaker at *Survivor Series 1996*?
    a. Kamala   c. Jake Roberts
    b. Mankind   d. Triple H

SURVIVOR SERIES 1997-1998

1. Vader eliminated three of the four Superstars on the Team Canada squad during *Survivor Series 1997*. Which member of the team did he *not* eliminate?
    a. Jim Neidhart   c. Phil Lafon
    b. Davey Boy Smith   d. Doug Furnas

2. Who won the Intercontinental Championship at *Survivor Series 1997*?
    a. Steve Austin   c. Triple H
    b. Owen Hart   d. The Rock

3. Who was the only survivor of the match between the Truth Commission and Disciples of the Apocalypse at *Survivor Series 1997*?
    a. Interrogator   c. Crush
    b. Sniper   d. 8 Ball

4. What member of Team USA walked out on his teammates at *Survivor Series 1997*?
    a. Steve Blackman
    b. Vader
    c. Goldust
    d. Marc Mero

5. Who was the only survivor of the Elimination match between Hawk, Animal, Ahmed Johnson, Ken Shamrock, and the Nation of Domination at *Survivor Series 1997?*
   a. Ahmed Johnson   c. D'Lo Brown
   b. Faarooq   d. Ken Shamrock

6. What city played host to *Survivor Series 1997?*
   a. Miami   c. Montreal
   b. Chicago   d. Cleveland

7. Who was *not* one of the Superstars The Rock faced en route to the finals of the WWE Championship tournament at *Survivor Series 1998?*
   a. Undertaker   c. Big Boss Man
   b. Kane   d. Ken Shamrock

8. Who was *not* one of the Superstars Mankind faced en route to the finals of the WWE Championship tournament at *Survivor Series 1998?*
   a. Al Snow   c. Jeff Jarrett
   b. Steve Austin   d. Duane Gill

9. Who won the WWE Women's Championship at *Survivor Series 1998?*
   a. Jacqueline   c. Ivory
   b. Sable   d. Debra

10. The New Age Outlaws defended the WWE World Tag
    Team Championship in a Triple Threat match at *Survivor
    Series 1998*. One of the teams they faced was the Head-
    bangers. What was the other?
    a. Brood
    b. D'Lo Brown & Mark
       Henry
    c. Legion of Doom
    d. Too Much

SURVIVOR SERIES 1999

1. Who teamed with Mankind to challenge the New Age
   Outlaws for the WWE World Tag Team Championship at
   Survivor Series 1999?
   a. Kane
   b. Ken Shamrock
   c. Al Snow
   d. Undertaker

2. Who got the pin when the team of the Fabulous Moolah,
   Mae Young, Tori & Debra defeated Ivory, Luna, Jacqueline
   & Terri Runnels at *Survivor Series 1999*?
   a. Fabulous Moolah
   b. Mae Young
   c. Tori
   d. Debra

3. Big Show attacked his partners backstage so he could
   compete alone at *Survivor Series 1999*. Who was *not*
   supposed to be on Big Show's team?
   a. Blue Meanie
   b. Steven Richards
   c. Funaki
   d. Taka Michinoku

4. Who successfully defended the WWE Intercontinental
   Championship at *Survivor Series 1999*?
   a. Val Venis   c. Chyna
   b. Chris Jericho   d. X-Pac

5. Whom did Kurt Angle defeat at *Survivor Series 1999*, his
   WWE Pay-Per-View debut?
   a. Tazz   c. Shawn Stasiak
   b. Goldust   d. Mark Henry

6. Who teamed with the Mean Street Posse for their match at
   Survivor Series 1999?
   a. Shane McMahon   c. Steve Blackman
   b. British Bulldog   d. Steven Richards

7. What tag team was the only one to survive when the
   Godfather & D'Lo Brown and the Headbangers faced the
   Dudley Boys and the Acolytes at *Survivor Series 1999*?
   a. Acolytes   c. Godfather & D'Lo Brown
   b. Dudley Boys   d. Headbangers

8. Who was the only survivor when the team of Too Cool and
   the Hollys won their match at *Survivor Series 1999*?
   a. Hardcore Holly   c. Grandmaster Sexay
   b. Crash Holly   d. Scotty 2 Hotty

9. Who replaced Steve Austin in the Triple Threat match for the WWE Championship at *Survivor Series 1999* when he was run down by a car?

   a. Undertaker   c. Big Show

   b. Mankind   d. Kane

10. Who was *not* pinned by Big Show during his One-on-Four Handicap match at *Survivor Series 1999*?

    a. Mideon   c. Big Boss Man

    b. Prince Albert   d. Viscera

SURVIVOR SERIES 2000–2001

1. What is the name of Kurt Angle's brother who got involved during Kurt's WWE Championship match against Undertaker at *Survivor Series 2000*?

   a. Robert   c. Eric

   b. Kyle   d. John

2. What was the result of the six-person Mixed Tag match between the teams of Steve Blackman, Crash Holly & Molly Holly and Test, Albert & Trish Stratus at *Survivor Series 2000*?

   a. Trish pinned Molly.

   b. Steve Blackman pinned Albert.

   c. Molly pinned Trish.

   d. Test pinned Crash Holly.

3. Who teamed with D-Generation X for their match against the Radicalz at *Survivor Series 2000*?
   - a. Kane
   - b. K-Kwik
   - c. Chris Jericho
   - d. Mankind

4. In what type of match did Steve Austin and Triple H compete at *Survivor Series 2000*?
   - a. Street Fight
   - b. Last Man Standing
   - c. No Disqualification
   - d. Steel Cage

5. Who was the only survivor when the Dudley Boys and the Hardys faced the Right to Censor and Edge & Christian at *Survivor Series 2000*?
   - a. Matt Hardy
   - b. Jeff Hardy
   - c. D-Von Dudley
   - d. Bubba Ray Dudley

6. The Rock eliminated three Superstars in the Winner Take All match at *Survivor Series 2001*. Who was *not* eliminated by The Rock?
   - a. Steve Austin
   - b. Rob Van Dam
   - c. Kurt Angle
   - d. Booker T

7. What member of Team WWE was eliminated by Shane McMahon in the Winner Take All match at *Survivor Series 2001*?
   - a. Kane
   - b. Undertaker
   - c. Big Show
   - d. Chris Jericho

8. Who won the Immunity Battle Royal at *Survivor Series 2001?*
   a. Billy Gunn   c. Test
   b. Hurricane   d. Tazz

9. Who was powerbombed by William Regal after his match with Tajiri at *Survivor Series 2001?*
   a. Debra   c. Torrie Wilson
   b. Stacy Keibler   d. Molly Holly

10. In what type of match did the Dudley Boys and Hardys unify the WWE Tag Team Championship and WCW Tag Team Championship at *Survivor Series 2001?*
   a. Ladder   c. TLC
   b. Tables   d. Steel Cage

SURVIVOR SERIES 2002–2003

1. In what type of match did Trish Stratus and Victoria compete for the Women's Championship at *Survivor Series 2002?*
   a. Submission   c. Bra and Panties
   b. Hardcore   d. Lumberjill

2. What duo won a Triple Threat Elimination match for the WWE Tag Team Championship at *Survivor Series 2002?*
   a. Edge & Rey Mysterio
   b. Los Guerreros
   c. Chris Benoit & Kurt Angle
   d. World's Greatest Tag Team

3. Who was the last Superstar remaining when Spike Dudley, Jeff Hardy, and Bubba Ray Dudley faced 3 Minute Warning and Rico in an Elimination Tables match at *Survivor Series 2002*?
   a. Bubba Ray Dudley
   b. Jamal
   c. Rosey
   d. Jeff Hardy

4. How many Superstars did reigning World Heavyweight Champion Triple H eliminate from the Elimination Chamber match at *Survivor Series 2002*?
   a. 0
   b. 1
   c. 2
   d. 3

5. Who won the WWE Cruiserweight Championship at *Survivor Series 2002*?
   a. Jamie Noble
   b. Matt Hardy
   c. Billy Kidman
   d. Tajiri

6. In what type of match did Shane McMahon and Kane compete at *Survivor Series 2003*?
   a. Greenwich Street Fight
   b. Inferno
   c. Last Man Standing
   d. Ambulance

7. Who was the only survivor when Team Bischoff met Team Austin at *Survivor Series 2003*?
   a. Shawn Michaels
   b. Rob Van Dam
   c. Chris Jericho
   d. Randy Orton

8. Who assisted Mr. McMahon in his Buried Alive match against Undertaker at *Survivor Series 2003*?
   a. Kane
   b. Mark Henry
   c. Big Show
   d. Bradshaw

9. Who successfully defended the WWE Women's Championship at *Survivor Series 2003*?
   a. Molly Holly
   b. Lita
   c. Ivory
   d. Victoria

10. Who left *Survivor Series 2003* as the World Heavyweight Champion?
    a. Triple H
    b. Shawn Michaels
    c. Goldberg
    d. Kane

SURVIVOR SERIES 2004–2005

1. Who was the only member of Eddie Guerrero's team eliminated when they faced Kurt Angle's team at *Survivor Series 2004*?
   a. Eddie Guerrero
   b. Big Show
   c. Rob Van Dam
   d. John Cena

2. Who won the Fatal Four Way match for the WWE Cruiserweight Championship at *Survivor Series 2004*?
   a. Billy Kidman
   b. Rey Mysterio
   c. Spike Dudley
   d. Chavo Guerrero

3. Who was the only survivor when Team Orton met Team
    Triple H at *Survivor Series 2004*?
    a. Randy Orton   c. Edge
    b. Triple H   d. Chris Jericho

4. Who challenged JBL for the WWE Championship at
    Survivor Series 2004?
    a. Undertaker   c. Carlito
    b. Booker T   d. Batista

5. Who successfully defended the WWE Intercontinental
    Championship at *Survivor Series 2004*?
    a. Jeff Hardy   c. Christian
    b. Shelton Benjamin   d. Orlando Jordan

6. In what type of match did Triple H and Ric Flair compete
    at *Survivor Series 2005*?
    a. Steel Cage   c. Last Man Standing
    b. Submission   d. First Blood

7. Who was the only survivor when Team *Raw* met Team
    SmackDown! at *Survivor Series 2005*?
    a. Shawn Michaels   c. Big Show
    b. Randy Orton   d. Batista

8. Who interfered in the Theodore Long–Eric Bischoff match
    at *Survivor Series 2005*, allowing Theodore Long to get the
    win?
    a. Eugene   c. Boogeyman
    b. Snitsky   d. Simon Dean

9. Who was the special guest referee when John Cena and Kurt Angle met for the WWE Championship at *Survivor Series 2005*?
   a. Carlito
   b. Daivari
   c. Edge
   d. Booker T

10. Who challenged Trish Stratus for the Women's Championship at *Survivor Series 2005*?
    a. Victoria
    b. Mickie James
    c. Ashley
    d. Melina

SURVIVOR SERIES 2006–2007

1. Who was the only survivor when a team of WWE Legends met the Spirit Squad in a traditional *Survivor Series* match at *Survivor Series 2006*?
   a. Ron Simmons
   b. Kenny
   c. Ric Flair
   d. Dusty Rhodes

2. What Diva had her final match at *Survivor Series 2006*?
   a. Lita
   b. Trish Stratus
   c. Stacy Keibler
   d. Fabulous Moolah

3. What member of John Cena's team survived *with* Cena when the team defeated Team Big Show at *Survivor Series 2006*?
   a. RVD
   b. Bobby Lashley
   c. Sabu
   d. Kane

4. In what type of match did Mr. Kennedy and Undertaker compete at *Survivor Series 2006*?
   - a. Last Ride
   - b. Casket
   - c. First Blood
   - d. Falls Count Anywhere

5. Who attacked Undertaker during his match with Mr. Kennedy at *Survivor Series 2006*?
   - a. Test
   - b. MVP
   - c. Finlay
   - d. Umaga

6. What member of Team DX eliminated two members of Team Rated RKO during their match at *Survivor Series 2006*?
   - a. Triple H
   - b. CM Punk
   - c. Jeff Hardy
   - d. Shawn Michaels

7. Who got the pin during the Ten Diva Tag match at *Survivor Series 2007*?
   - a. Victoria
   - b. Mickie James
   - c. Beth Phoenix
   - d. Michelle McCool

8. Who was the first member of Team Umaga eliminated during their match against Team Triple H at *Survivor Series 2007*?
   - a. Mr. Kennedy
   - b. Big Daddy V
   - c. MVP
   - d. Finlay

9. What was the result of the World Tag Team Championship match featuring Hardcore Holly & Cody Rhodes challenging Lance Cade & Trevor Murdoch at *Survivor Series 2007*?
   a. Murdoch pinned Rhodes.
   b. Rhodes pinned Cade.
   c. Cade pinned Holly.
   d. Holly pinned Murdoch.

10. Who interfered in the Great Khali versus Hornswoggle match at *Survivor Series 2007*?
    a. Shane McMahon
    b. Finlay
    c. Carlito
    d. CM Punk

SECTION XVII
ARMAGEDDON

ARMAGEDDON 1999

1. In what type of match did Triple H and Mr. McMahon
    compete at *Armageddon 1999*?
    - a. Street Fight
    - b. Steel Cage
    - c. No Holds Barred
    - d. Sledgehammer on a Pole

2. Who challenged Big Show for the WWE Championship at
    Armageddon 1999?
    - a. Kurt Angle
    - b. Big Boss Man
    - c. Rikishi
    - d. Undertaker

3. Who won a Four Corners Evening Gown match to win the
    Women's Championship at *Armageddon 1999*?
    - a. Ivory
    - b. B.B.
    - c. Jacqueline
    - d. Miss Kitty

4. What tag team won a shot at the Tag Team Championship
    at *Royal Rumble 2000* by virtue of winning a Tag Team
    Battle Royal at *Armageddon 1999*?
    - a. Headbangers
    - b. Mean Street Posse
    - c. Acolytes
    - d. Godfather & Mark Henry

5. Who accompanied Chyna to the ring for her match for the
    Intercontinental Championship against Chris Jericho at
    Armageddon 1999?
    - a. Triple H
    - b. Eddie Guerrero
    - c. Miss Kitty
    - d. Billy Gunn

6. Who interfered in the WWE World Tag Team Championship match at *Armageddon 1999*, costing the Rock 'n' Sock Connection a chance at the championship?

   a. X-Pac

   b. Undertaker

   c. Al Snow

   d. Test

7. Who won a Triple Threat match for the WWE European Championship at *Armageddon 1999*?

   a. William Regal

   b. Val Venis

   c. British Bulldog

   d. D'Lo Brown

8. What member of D-Generation X faced Kane in a Steel Cage match at *Armageddon 1999*?

   a. Triple H

   b. Billy Gunn

   c. Road Dogg

   d. X-Pac

9. What big man teamed with Viscera to face Hardcore & Crash Holly at *Armageddon 1999*?

   a. Yokozuna

   b. Bam Bam Bigelow

   c. Rikishi

   d. Vader

10. Who were the special guest referees for the Four Corners Evening Gown match for the Women's Championship at *Armageddon 1999*?

    a. Jim Ross and Jerry Lawler

    b. Fabulous Moolah and Mae Young

    c. Bobby Heenan and Gene Okerlund

    d. Val Venis and Godfather

ARMAGEDDON 2000–2002

1. When Eddie Guerrero, Dean Malenko & Perry Saturn met the Hardys & Lita in a Six-Man Elimination Tag match at *Armageddon 2000,* who was *not* eliminated?
   a. Matt Hardy
   b. Lita
   c. Dean Malenko
   d. Eddie Guerrero

2. What tag team won the Fatal Four Way match for the World Tag Team Championship at *Armageddon 2000?*
   a. Road Dogg & K-Kwik
   b. Right to Censor
   c. Dudley Boys
   d. Edge & Christian

3. When Kurt Angle won the Six-Man Hell in a Cell match for the WWE Championship at *Armageddon 2000,* whom did he pin?
   a. Rikishi
   b. Undertaker
   c. The Rock
   d. Triple H

4. In what type of match did Chris Jericho and Kane compete at *Armageddon 2000?*
   a. Last Man Standing
   b. Inferno
   c. Street Fight
   d. Falls Count Anywhere

5. Who defeated Chyna in an intergender match at *Armageddon 2000?*
   a. Billy Gunn
   b. Goodfather
   c. Val Venis
   d. Hardcore Holly

6. In the Three Stages of Hell match at *Armageddon 2002*, at
    what stage did Shawn Michaels win?
    a. street fight
    b. submission
    c. steel cage
    d. ladder

7. What tag team won the Fatal Four Way Elimination match
    for the World Tag Team Championship at *Armageddon
    2002*?
    a. Lance Storm & William Regal
    b. Chris Jericho & Christian
    c. Booker T & Goldust
    d. Dudley Boys

8. Who won the WWE Championship at *Armageddon 2002*?
    a. Undertaker
    b. Kurt Angle
    c. Big Show
    d. Brock Lesnar

9. What Diva retained the Women's Championship in a
    Triple Threat match at *Armageddon 2002*?
    a. Jacqueline
    b. Victoria
    c. Trish Stratus
    d. Lita

10. What was the result of the match between Edge and
    A-Train at *Armageddon 2002*?
    a. Edge pinned A-Train.
    b. A-Train pinned Edge.
    c. Both men were counted out.
    d. A-Train was disqualified.

ARMAGEDDON 2003–2004

1. Who managed Mark Henry for his match against Booker T at *Armageddon 2003*?
   - a. Jacqueline
   - b. Theodore Long
   - c. Rico
   - d. Faarooq

2. What team won the Tag Team Turmoil match at *Armageddon 2003*?
   - a. La Resistance
   - b. Batista & Ric Flair
   - c. Rosey & Hurricane
   - d. Dudley Boys

3. Who was the special guest referee for the Intercontinental Championship match between Randy Orton and Rob Van Dam at *Armageddon 2003*?
   - a. Ric Flair
   - b. Honky Tonk Man
   - c. Mick Foley
   - d. Tommy Dreamer

4. Who was the World Heavyweight Champion heading in to *Armageddon 2003*?
   - a. Goldberg
   - b. Triple H
   - c. Shawn Michaels
   - d. Kane

5. Who recorded the pin in the Intergender Tag Team match between Christian & Chris Jericho and Lita & Trish Stratus at *Armageddon 2003*?
   - a. Christian
   - b. Jericho
   - c. Trish Stratus
   - d. Lita

6. When JBL retained the WWE Championship in a Fatal Four Way match at *Armageddon 2004*, whom did he pin?
   a. Eddie Guerrero
   b. Booker T
   c. Undertaker
   d. Heidenreich

7. Who got the pin when Big Show faced Kurt Angle, Luther Reigns, and Mark Jindrak in a Three-on-One Handicap match at *Armageddon 2004*?
   a. Big Show
   b. Kurt Angle
   c. Luther Reigns
   d. Mark Jindrak

8. Who won the WWE Cruiserweight Championship at *Armageddon 2004*?
   a. Spike Dudley
   b. Hurricane
   c. Funaki
   d. Hardcore Holly

9. Who challenged John Cena for the WWE United States Championship in a Street Fight at *Armageddon 2004*?
   a. Carlito
   b. Jesus
   c. Orlando Jordan
   d. Kenzo Suzuki

10. Who defeated Santa Claus at *Armageddon 2004*?
    a. Kurt Angle
    b. Daniel Puder
    c. Rene Dupree
    d. JBL

ARMAGEDDON 2005–2006

1. Who won the WWE Cruiserweight Championship at *Armageddon 2005*?
   a. Juventud
   b. Gregory Helms
   c. Chavo Guerrero
   d. Kid Kash

2. Who got the pin when MNM faced the Mexicools at *Armageddon 2005*?
   a. Joey Mercury
   b. Super Crazy
   c. Psicosis
   d. Johnny Nitro

3. What team of *Raw* Superstars faced Batista & Rey Mysterio at *Armageddon 2005*?
   a. Chris Masters & Carlito
   b. Big Show & Kane
   c. Edge & Ric Flair
   d. John Cena & Shawn Michaels

4. What former World Champion defeated Matt Hardy at *Armageddon 2005*?
   a. JBL
   b. Undertaker
   c. Booker T
   d. Randy Orton

5. Who teamed with William Regal to face Bobby Lashley in a Handicap match at *Armageddon 2005*?
   a. Funaki
   b. Finlay
   c. Paul Birchill
   d. Eugene

6. In what type of match did Undertaker and Mr. Kennedy compete at *Armageddon 2006*?
   - a. Buried Alive
   - b. Casket
   - c. Last Ride
   - d. Hell in a Cell

7. Who recorded the pin when Batista & John Cena teamed to face King Booker & Finlay at *Armageddon 2006*?
   - a. Batista
   - b. John Cena
   - c. King Booker
   - d. Finlay

8. Who won the Ladder match for the WWE Tag Team Championship at *Armageddon 2006*?
   - a. Paul London & Brian Kendrick
   - b. William Regal & Dave Taylor
   - c. MNM
   - d. Hardy Boys

9. In what type of match did Kane and MVP compete at *Armageddon 2006*?
   - a. Last Man Standing
   - b. Inferno
   - c. Steel Cage
   - d. Falls Count Anywhere

10. Who challenged Gregory Helms for the WWE Cruiserweight Championship at *Armageddon 2006*?
   - a. Scotty 2 Hotty
   - b. Chavo Guerrero
   - c. Jimmy Wang Yang
   - d. Funaki

ANSWERS

SECTION I. *ROYAL RUMBLE*

THE FIRST *ROYAL RUMBLE*

1. b. Jim Duggan
2. d. Hamilton, Ontario
3. b. 20
4. a. Tito Santana
5. b. Bret Hart
6. b. Jumping Bomb Angels
7. a. Islanders won 2–0.
8. b. Ricky Steamboat
9. a. One Man Gang
10. d. Andre the Giant

ROYAL RUMBLE 1989–1990

1. b. Demolition
2. b. Warlord
3. c. 9
4. b. Big John Studd
5. a. Mr. Perfect
6. b. Ted DiBiase
7. c. "I Quit"

8. c. Mr. Perfect
9. d. Double
        disqualification.
10. b. Jim Duggan

ROYAL RUMBLE 1991

1. a. Randy Savage
2. c. Mountie
3. c. Bret Hart
4. a. DiBiase pinned Dusty
        Rhodes.
5. c. Randy Savage
6. d. Rick Martel
7. c. Orient Express
8. a. Hulk Hogan
9. c. Earthquake
10. b. Barbarian

ROYAL RUMBLE 1992–1993

1. b. Ted DiBiase
2. c. 3
3. d. Roddy Piper
4. b. Jamison
5. c. Hulk Hogan
6. c. Tito Santana
7. c. Giant Gonzales
8. d. Bob Backlund
9. a. Yokozuna
10. c. Razor Ramon

ROYAL RUMBLE 1994–1995

1. c. Irwin R. Shyster
2. b. Yokozuna locked
        Undertaker in the
        casket.
3. b. 7
4. c. Bam Bam Bigelow
5. c. The referee stopped
        the match due
        to injury to
        Bret.
6. d. The match was
        declared a draw.
7. a. Jeff Jarrett
8. d. Bob Holly & the
        1-2-3 Kid
9. b. Razor Ramon
10. b. Shawn Michaels

ROYAL RUMBLE 1996–1997

1. c. Diesel
2. a. 0
3. b. Duke Droese
4. b. Vader
5. c. Goldust
6. c. Smokin' Gunns
7. c. Shawn Michaels
8. c. Goldust
9. d. Bret Hart
10. b. 9

ROYAL RUMBLE 1998-1999

1. c. The Rock
2. d. Owen Hart
3. d. Casket
4. c. Sunny
5. b. The Rock
6. b. 1
7. b. Chyna
8. c. Strap
9. d. Mankind
10. a. Ken Shamrock

ROYAL RUMBLE 2000-2001

1. c. Hardcore Holly
2. b. Rikishi
3. c. Acolytes
4. c. Street Fight
5. b. Mae Young
6. b. Steven Richards
7. c. 11
8. c. Trish Stratus
9. b. The Rock
10. c. Chris Jericho

ROYAL RUMBLE 2002-2003

1. b. Maven
2. b. Kurt Angle
3. c. The Rock
4. b. Flair made Mr. McMahon submit.

5. b. Jacqueline
6. d. Brock Lesnar
7. a. Scott Steiner won by disqualification.
8. d. Shawn Michaels
9. c. Undertaker
10. a. Dudley Boys

ROYAL RUMBLE 2004-2005

1. c. Spike Dudley
2. c. Hardcore Holly
3. c. Mick Foley
4. c. A double countout.
5. b. Evolution
6. b. Scotty 2 Hotty
7. c. Nunzio
8. d. John Cena
9. b. Triple Threat
10. b. Heidenreich

ROYAL RUMBLE 2006-2007

1. b. Gregory Helms
2. a. Rey Mysterio
3. c. Shane McMahon
4. b. Trish Stratus
5. b. Mark Henry
6. d. #30

7. b. King Booker

8. d. Lashley won by countout.

9. d. Last Man Standing

10. b. CM Punk

SECTION II. GOLD RUSH

INTERCONTINENTAL CHAMPIONSHIP

1. d. Pat Patterson
2. c. Chris Jericho
3. d. Italy
4. c. Ricky Steamboat
5. c. Mr. Perfect
6. a. Owen Hart
7. d. Dean Douglas
8. c. Pedro Morales
9. d. Chris Jericho and Chyna
10. b. Christian

WWE CRUISERWEIGHT CHAMPIONSHIP

1. c. Tajiri
2. a. Rey Mysterio
3. c. Chavo Classic
4. d. Vickie Guerrero
5. a. Nunzio
6. b. Jamie Noble
7. b. Gregory Helms
8. b. 3
9. c. Tajiri
10. c. 8

EUROPEAN CHAMPIONSHIP

1. b. British Bulldog
2. a. D'Lo Brown
3. d. Germany
4. a. Shawn Michaels
5. c. *WrestleMania XIV*
6. d. William Regal
7. b. Rob Van Dam
8. d. Triple H
9. d. Chris Jericho
10. c. Matt Hardy

HARDCORE CHAMPIONSHIP

1. b. Crash Holly
2. d. Lita
3. a. Bradshaw
4. d. Raven
5. c. Mr. Perfect
6. b. Tommy Dreamer
7. b. Rob Van Dam
8. d. Big Boss Man
9. d. Big Boss Man
10. c. Pete Gas

WWE CHAMPIONSHIP

1. c. Kurt Angle
2. d. Ivan Koloff
3. b. Sgt. Slaughter
4. a. Andre the Giant
5. d. *Survivor Series*
6. a. The Rock
7. a. 1
8. c. Brock Lesnar
9. d. *New Year's Revolution*
10. c. Diesel

WWE WOMEN'S CHAMPIONSHIP

1. b. Alundra Blayze
2. d. Fabulous Moolah
3. d. Jacqueline
4. c. Gail Kim
5. c. 7
6. d. Evening Gown
7. d. Mickie James
8. d. *Great American Bash*
9. c. Harvey Wippleman
10. d. Trish Stratus

SECTION III. *NO WAY OUT*

NO WAY OUT 1998–2001

1. b. Bradshaw
2. d. Taka Michinoku
3. a. Ken Shamrock
4. c. Savio Vega
5. c. Kurt Angle
6. c. No Holds Barred
7. b. Terri Runnels
8. c. William Regal
9. c. Kat
10. a. The Rock

NO WAY OUT 2002–2004

1. b. APA
2. a. Brass Knuckles on a Pole

3. b. Steve Austin
4. b. Matt Hardy
5. c. Steve Austin
6. b. William Regal & Lance Storm
7. b. Blindfold
8. b. John Cena
9. b. Rikishi
10. b. Jorge Paez

NO WAY OUT 2005–2007

1. b. Paul London
2. c. Kurt Angle
3. d. Gregory Helms
4. b. Finlay

5. c. Tatanka

6. c. Randy Orton

7. b. Ashley

8. a. John Cena

9. c. Chavo Guerrero

10. a. Finlay

SECTION IV. *WRESTLEMANIA*

WRESTLEMANIA

1. c. New York
2. c. Jimmy Snuka
3. b. Capt. Lou Albano
4. b. Tito Santana
5. d. Muhammad Ali
6. b. Hulk Hogan pinned Paul Orndorff.
7. c. 9 seconds
8. a. Leilani Kai
9. d. Greg Valentine
10. b. Bobby Heenan

WRESTLEMANIA 2

1. c. Philadelphia Spectrum
2. d. Tommy Lasorda
3. a. Ozzie Osbourne
4. c. Greg Valentine
5. b. fourth
6. a. Ray Charles
7. c. Corp. Kirschner
8. d. Velvet McIntyre
9. d. George Steele
10. d. Jimmy Hart

WRESTLEMANIA III

1. c. Tito Santana
2. a. Jake Roberts
3. c. Detroit
4. d. Bobby Heenan
5. c. ring bell
6. c. Can-Am Connection
7. c. Adrian Adonis
8. d. Junkyard Dog
9. a. Tom Zenk
10. d. 93,173

WRESTLEMANIA IV

1. a. Bad News Brown
2. d. Islanders
3. c. Gladys Knight
4. c. 14
5. d. Dino Bravo
6. b. Bob Uecker
7. b. quarterfinals
8. c. Demolition
9. a. Ultimate Warrior
10. c. Brutus Beefcake

WRESTLEMANIA V

1. b. New Jersey
2. d. Morton Downey Jr.
3. c. Big John Studd
4. a. Brooklyn Brawler
5. d. Ultimate Warrior
6. b. Jim Duggan
7. c. Frenchy Martin
8. a. Akeem pinned Shawn Michaels.
9. c. in a neutral corner
10. b. Demolition

WRESTLEMANIA VI

1. c. Genius
2. b. Demolition
3. c. Robert Goulet
4. d. pink
5. a. Boston Crab
6. b. Sato
7. a. Mr. Fuji
8. c. Jimmy Snuka
9. b. Ultimate Challenge
10. c. Sapphire pinned Sherri.

WRESTLEMANIA VII

1. a. Los Angeles
2. b. Andre the Giant
3. c. Alex Trebek
4. b. Undertaker
5. a. Randy Savage
6. d. Hart Foundation
7. a. pinfall
8. c. Blindfold
9. a. Slick
10. d. Virgil

WRESTLEMANIA VIII

1. d. Skinner
2. d. Paul Ellering
3. b. Papa Shango
4. a. Virgil
5. b. Bret Hart
6. d. Harvey Wippleman
7. b. Tatanka
8. c. Money Inc.
9. d. Mr. Perfect
10. b. 2

WRESTLEMANIA IX

1. c. Mega Maniacs
2. c. Jim Ross
3. a. Afa
4. d. Tatanka
5. c. Bob Backlund
6. c. Las Vegas
7. b. Shawn Michaels
8. b. Lex Luger pinned Mr. Perfect.

9. c. Giant Gonzales

10. d. black and gold

WRESTLEMANIA X

1. c. Falls Count Anywhere
2. b. Johnny Polo
3. b. Adam Bomb
4. d. Mr. Perfect
5. c. Little Richard
6. c. Bret Hart
7. a. Madison Square Garden
8. d. Alundra Blayze
9. b. Mo
10. a. Roddy Piper

WRESTLEMANIA XI

1. d. MLB
2. b. Andre Tippett
3. d. 1-2-3 Kid
4. c. Pamela Anderson
5. c. "I Quit"
6. c. Owen Hart & Yokuzuna
7. c. Uncle Zebekiah
8. c. Roddy Piper
9. c. Connecticut
10. b. "Whatta Man"

WRESTLEMANIA XII

1. c. Gorilla Monsoon
2. b. Vader
3. d. Savio Vega
4. a. Sable
5. b. Diesel
6. d. Bodydonnas
7. c. Anaheim
8. c. He stripped Goldust down, and Goldust walked out.
9. a. Mr. Fuji
10. d. Million Dollar Dream

WRESTLEMANIA 13

1. a. Ken Shamrock
2. c. New Blackjacks
3. b. Vader
4. b. No-Disqualification
5. a. D'Lo Brown
6. a. 2
7. d. The Rock
8. c. Ahmed Johnson
9. d. Chicago
10. c. Honky Tonk Man

WRESTLEMANIA XIV

1. b. LOD 2000
2. c. Sable pinned Luna.

3. b. Sgt. Slaughter
4. c. Dumpster
5. d. Pete Rose
6. c. Boston
7. c. Taka Michinoku
8. b. New Midnight Express
9. a. The Rock
10. d. Mike Tyson

WRESTLEMANIA XV

1. c. Shawn Michaels
2. b. Road Dogg
3. c. Butterbean
4. a. Hardcore Holly
5. b. Mankind
6. c. San Diego Chicken
7. b. Test
8. c. Nicole Bass
9. c. No Disqualification
10. a. Owen Hart & Jeff Jarrett

WRESTLEMANIA XVI

1. b. Ice-T
2. c. Triple H
3. a. Chris Jericho
4. b. Tazz
5. d. Val Venis
6. b. Big Show

7. a. Edge & Christian
8. d. Chyna
9. c. Head Cheese
10. a. Hardcore Holly

WRESTLEMANIA X-SEVEN

1. d. Iron Sheik
2. b. Sign Guy Dudley
3. b. Chyna
4. c. Eddie Guerrero
5. d. Kane
6. c. Mick Foley
7. b. Last Ride
8. d. Mr. McMahon
9. b. Houston . . . We Have a Problem
10. a. Edge & Christian

WRESTLEMANIA X8

1. d. Diamond Dallas Page
2. b. 5
3. d. Jazz
4. c. Kane
5. d. Billy & Chuck
6. b. Arn Anderson
7. a. William Regal
8. c. Stephanie McMahon
9. b. Scott Hall
10. c. Toronto

WRESTLEMANIA XIX

1. b. Seattle
2. c. 3
3. b. Roddy Piper
4. c. Brock Lesnar
5. c. Booker T
6. d. Matt Hardy
7. c. Pillow Fight
8. b. Nathan Jones
9. b. Ric Flair
10. c. Trish Stratus

WRESTLEMANIA XX

1. d. United States
2. a. Randy Orton
3. c. Rikishi & Scotty 2 Hotty
4. c. Molly Holly
5. d. Eddie Guerrero
6. b. Chavo Guerrero
7. b. Triple H
8. c. Donald Trump
9. b. Kane
10. b. Goldberg pinned Lesnar.

WRESTLEMANIA 21

1. d. Big Show
2. c. Rhyno
3. a. Hulk Hogan

4. c. Steve Austin
5. b. Trish Stratus
6. c. Superstar Billy Graham
7. a. Motörhead
8. b. *Gladiator*
9. d. Eddie Guerrero
10. d. JBL

WRESTLEMANIA 22

1. a. Big Time
2. b. JBL
3. c. Rob Van Dam
4. b. Trish Stratus
5. a. Michelle Williams
6. d. Chicago
7. b. JBL
8. c. Torrie Wilson
9. a. Casket
10. d. Triple H

WRESTLEMANIA 23

1. c. Shelton Benjamin
2. a. United States
3. d. Mr. Kennedy
4. c. Rob Van Dam
5. d. Lumberjill
6. b. Steve Austin

7. c. STFU

8. a. Miz

9. d. Ford Field

10. c. Kane

SECTION V. *BACKLASH*

BACKLASH 1999–2000

1. a. Triple H and
   X-Pac

2. a. Shane McMahon

3. c. Boiler Room
   Brawl

4. a. Debra

5. d. Viscera

6. c. The Rock

7. b. European

8. c. Trish Stratus

9. b. Tazz

10. a. Dean Malenko

BACKLASH 2001–2002

1. b. Matt Hardy

2. a. K-Kwik

3. c. Chris Jericho

4. b. Triple H

5. c. Raven

6. b. Ric Flair

7. c. Torrie Wilson

8. a. Jazz

9. c. Eddie Guerrero

10. b. Undertaker

BACKLASH 2003

1. d. Chief Morley

2. c. The Rock

3. c. John Cena

4. c. Sean O'Haire

5. c. Charlie Haas pinned
   Chavo Guerrero.

6. c. Booker T

7. c. Trish Stratus

8. a. Triple H pinned Kevin
   Nash.

9. c. Theodore Long

10. b. Big Show pinned Rey
   Mysterio.

BACKLASH 2004–2005

1. c. Tajiri

2. a. Jericho pinned
   Christian.

3. b. Victoria

4. c. Shelton Benjamin

5. b. Mick Foley

6. d. Viscera

7. c. Hurricane & Rosey

8. d. Shelton Benjamin

9. c. Last Man Standing
10. d. Shawn Michaels

BACKLASH 2006–2007

1. c. The match was
        declared no contest.
2. c. Mr. McMahon pinned
        Shawn Michaels.
3. b. Rob Van Dam

4. c. Trish Stratus won by
        disqualification.
5. c. Triple Threat
6. d. Matt Hardy pinned
        Trevor Murdoch.
7. c. Mickie James
8. c. Last Man Standing
9. b. Randy Orton
10. c. Mr. McMahon

SECTION VI. *JUDGMENT DAY*

JUDGMENT DAY 1998–2002

1. c. Steve Austin
2. b. WWE European
3. d. Ken Shamrock
4. c. Triple H won 6–5.
5. d. Double Tables
6. a. Shawn Michaels
7. c. Kurt Angle
8. b. Chain
9. d. Triple H
10. c. Justin Credible

JUDGMENT DAY 2002–2003

1. a. Undertaker
2. b. Paul Heyman
3. c. Rikishi & Rico
4. d. Ric Flair &
        Big Show

5. a. Stacy Keibler
6. b. Christian
7. c. Jazz
8. c. Tazz
9. b. Stretcher
10. c. Nash won by
        disqualification.

JUDGMENT DAY 2004–2005

1. b. Billy Gunn
2. a. Jacqueline
3. c. Rene Dupree
4. b. JBL won by
        disqualification.
5. c. Rey Mysterio
6. b. Charlie Haas
7. a. Orlando Jordan
8. d. "I Quit"

9. b. Paul London

10. b. Rey Mysterio won by disqualification.

JUDGMENT DAY 2002-2003

1. c. Great Khali
2. c. Johnny Nitro
3. b. Super Crazy
4. c. Rey Mysterio pinned JBL
5. a. Jillian Hall
6. b. Shane McMahon
7. c. The referee stopped the match.
8. b. Jeff Hardy pinned Lance Cade.
9. c. MVP
10. d. Cena made Great Khali submit.

SECTION VII. *ONE NIGHT STAND*

ONE NIGHT STAND 2005-2006

1. c. Mick Foley
2. d. Spike Dudley
3. b. JBL
4. d. Sandman
5. a. Awesome pinned Tanaka.
6. b. Shane Douglas
7. b. The Dudley Boys pinned Tommy Dreamer after putting him through a flaming table.
8. b. Eric Bischoff
9. b. Balls Mahoney
10. b. Beulah

ONE NIGHT STAND 2006-2007

1. d. The match was declared no contest.
2. c. Edge
3. a. Angle made Orton submit.
4. c. Pudding
5. d. Lumberjack
6. b. World's Greatest Tag Team
7. a. Kevin Thorn
8. c. Jacksonville
9. b. Rob Van Dam
10. a. Falls Count Anywhere

SECTION VIII. *VENGEANCE*

VENGEANCE 2001–2002

1. a. Lita
2. d. Stacy Keibler
3. b. Albert
4. b. Booker T
5. b. Steve Austin
6. d. Lance Storm & Christian
7. c. Brock Lesnar
8. a. Undertaker
9. b. No Disqualification
10. b. Billy Kidman

VENGEANCE 2003–2004

1. b. Bradshaw
2. d. He has only one leg.
3. a. A-Train
4. b. Torrie Wilson
5. b. Eddie Guerrero
6. c. Ric Flair & Eugene
7. d. Victoria
8. b. Jonathan Coachman
9. a. Randy Orton
10. b. Matt Hardy

VENGEANCE 2005–2006

1. b. Viscera
2. d. Christy Hemme
3. a. Christian
4. b. Snitsky
5. d. Hell in a Cell
6. c. Flair won 2–0.
7. d. Johnny Nitro
8. c. Extreme Lumberjack
9. c. Spirit Squad
10. b. Kane

VENGEANCE 2007

1. c. Candice Michelle
2. b. Mick Foley
3. c. Sgt. Slaughter
4. d. Ric Flair
5. c. Johnny Nitro
6. a. Santino Marella
7. d. Batista was counted out.
8. c. Cade & Murdoch
9. c. Houston
10. b. Chavo Guerrero

SECTION IX. *GREAT AMERICAN BASH*

GREAT AMERICAN BASH 2004-2005

1. b. Rob Van Dam
2. a. Dudley Boys
3. c. Rey Mysterio
4. b. Texas Bullrope
5. c. Sable
6. b. Orlando Jordan
7. c. Candice Michelle
8. b. Psicosis
9. c. Muhammad Hassan
10. d. Batista was disqualified.

GREAT AMERICAN BASH 2006-2007

1. c. Ashley
2. c. William Regal
3. d. Big Show
4. b. Pit Bulls
5. c. Batista was disqualified.
6. b. Hornswoggle
7. d. Singapore Cane on a Pole
8. a. Bobby Lashley
9. c. Dusty Rhodes
10. c. Great Khali

SECTION X. SUPER STIPULATIONS

UNIQUE MATCHES

1. b. *Great American Bash*
2. c. Undertaker
3. d. Mankind
4. b. Owen Hart
5. d. Crash Holly
6. b. Easter Bunny
7. c. *SummerSlam*
8. c. Texas Death
9. b. Submission
10. c. XXXIII

ELIMINATION CHAMBER

1. c. *Survivor Series*
2. a. Shawn Michaels
3. c. Shawn Michaels and Chris Jericho
4. d. Batista
5. b. Test
6. b. stop sign
7. d. Kurt Angle
8. c. Carlito

9. a. Goldberg
10. b. Kevin Nash

HELL IN A CELL

1. b. Big Boss Man
2. d. Kurt Angle
3. b. *Badd Blood*
4. b. Triple H

5. d. Batista
6. a. Triple H pinned Mr. McMahon.
7. c. Randy Orton
8. b. Mick Foley
9. b. Triple H vs. Batista
10. d. Brock Lesnar

SECTION XI. *SUMMERSLAM*

THE FIRST *SUMMERSLAM*

1. c. Ultimate Warrior
2. b. Jesse Ventura
3. d. Jake Roberts
4. d. Jim Duggan
5. a. Ken Patera
6. c. New York
7. d. Baron
8. b. Hercules Hernandez
9. c. A time-limit draw.
10. c. Big Boss Man

SUMMERSLAM 1989–1990

1. b. Tito Santana
2. b. Ultimate Warrior
3. b. Smash pinned Akeem.
4. d. Zeus

5. c. Arn Anderson pinned Bret Hart.
6. b. Steel Cage
7. c. forfeit
8. d. Hart Foundation won 2–1.
9. b. Big Boss Man
10. c. Big Boss Man

SUMMERSLAM 1991–1992

1. a. Mr. Perfect
2. b. Sid Justice
3. c. Jail House
4. b. WWE
5. b. Andre the Giant
6. c. Ultimate Warrior
7. c. Both men were counted out.
8. b. Lennox Lewis

9. c. Genius
10. b. Kamala

SUMMERSLAM 1993–1994

1. b. Tatanka
2. b. Luger won by countout.
3. c. Heavenly Bodies
4. d. countout
5. c. Rest in Peace
6. d. Diesel
7. b. Tatanka
8. c. Bull Nakano
9. b. Ted DiBiase
10. c. Jim Neidhart

SUMMERSLAM 1995–1996

1. d. Hart won by disqualification.
2. b. Kama
3. b. Hardcore Holly
4. b. Razor Ramon
5. a. Harvey Wippleman
6. a. Smokin' Gunns
7. d. Yokozuna
8. a. Mark Henry
9. c. TKO
10. a. Vader

SUMMERSLAM 1997–1998

1. b. Shawn Michaels
2. c. never wrestle in the United States again
3. d. Goldust
4. a. Steel Cage
5. c. Ken Shamrock
6. a. Golga
7. a. Austin pinned Undertaker.
8. b. Edge
9. b. Hair vs. Hair
10. c. Kane

SUMMERSLAM 1999

1. c. kendo stick
2. a. Al Snow
3. b. Acolytes
4. c. Ivory
5. c. Mark Henry
6. b. Jesse Ventura
7. b. Undertaker pinned X-Pac.
8. a. Test pinned Shane.
9. a. Kiss My Ass
10. d. Mankind

SUMMERSLAM 2000–2001

1. b. Chyna
2. c. Stinkface

3. a.   The Rock
4. c.   Steve Blackman
5. a.   Steve Richards
6. d.   Edge
7. c.   Steel Cage
8. a.   The Rock
9. c.   Spike Dudley
10. c.   Rob Van Dam

SUMMERSLAM 2002–2003

1. d.   Brock Lesnar
2. a.   Test
3. c.   Rob Van Dam
4. d.   Unsanctioned Street Fight
5. b.   Un-Americans
6. c.   Eddie Guerrero
7. b.   Kurt Angle
8. c.   No Holds Barred
9. b.   Shane McMahon
10. b.   Sable

SUMMERSLAM 2004–2005

1. a.   JBL won by disqualification.

2. d.   Christian
3. b.   Kane
4. c.   Diva Dodgeball
5. a.   Randy Orton
6. b.   Hogan pinned Michaels.
7. c.   Christy Hemme
8. c.   Ladder
9. c.   Chris Jericho
10. c.   JBL

SUMMERSLAM 2006–2007

1. c.   "I Quit"
2. d.   Carlito
3. b.   Edge pinned Cena.
4. d.   Batista won by disqualification.
5. c.   Randy Orton
6. d.   Beth Phoenix
7. c.   Jeff Hardy
8. b.   beer drinking
9. a.   Great Khali
10. d.   John Morrison

SECTION XII. *UNFORGIVEN*

UNFORGIVEN 1998–1999

1. c.   Sable
2. c.   New Midnight Express

3. c.   Inferno
4. c.   Dude Love
5. a.   European

6. b. The Rock
7. a. Steve Austin
8. c. Al Snow
9. c. Brooklyn Brawler
10. c. Chyna

UNFORGIVEN 2000-2001

1. d. Steve Blackman
2. c. Strap
3. c. The Rock
4. b. Mick Foley
5. a. Val Venis
6. b. Rikishi
7. b. Dudley Boys
8. c. KroniK
9. b. Booker T
10. c. Rhyno

UNFORGIVEN 2002-2003

1. a. Kane
2. d. Both men were disqualified.
3. b. Molly Holly
4. c. Rob Van Dam
5. c. Chris Jericho
6. b. Coach pinned J.R.
7. b. Christian

8. b. Stacy Keibler
9. c. Lita pinned Molly Holly.
10. c. Goldberg

UNFORGIVEN 2004-2005

1. d. No Disqualification
2. b. Chris Jericho
3. c. Mr. McMahon
4. b. Tyson Tomko
5. c. La Resistance
6. b. Angle won by disqualification.
7. a. Trish Stratus
8. c. Steel Cage
9. d. Ric Flair
10. c. Chavo Guerrero

UNFORGIVEN 2006-2007

1. d. John Cena
2. c. Both men were counted out.
3. c. Lita
4. d. Spirit Squad
5. c. Jeff Hardy
6. b. Randy Orton won by disqualification.
7. b. Mark Henry
8. a. Beth Phoenix

9. b. Carlito could not be
         disqualified.

10. c. Matt Hardy pinned
         Deuce.

SECTION XIII. FORMER EVENTS

IN YOUR HOUSE

1. b. Savio Vega
2. c. Syracuse, NY
3. c. Diesel
4. b. Shawn Michaels
5. d. Bret Hart
6. d. Diesel
7. d. Mankind
8. d. Owen Hart
9. a. Headbangers
10. c. Big Show

NEW YEAR'S REVOLUTION

1. b. Maven
2. d. Muhammad
        Hassan
3. c. Shawn Michaels
4. c. Ashley
5. c. Edge
6. b. Viscera
7. d. Steel Cage
8. a. Cryme Tyme
9. d. The match was
        declared no contest.
10. b. Victoria

KING OF THE RING 1987–1993

1. d. King Kong Bundy
2. b. Tito Santana
3. b. Bret Hart
4. a. Providence
5. c. Yokozuna
6. b. Mr. Perfect
7. a. Billy Gunn
8. d. Crush
9. c. Bam Bam Bigelow
10. b. Bret Hart

KING OF THE RING 1994–1996

1. c. Roddy Piper
2. b. Jim Neidhart
3. b. Mabel
4. b. Bam Bam Bigelow
5. d. Hart won by
        submission.
6. c. Ahmed Johnson
7. b. Mr. Perfect
8. b. Marc Mero
9. c. Godwinns
10. d. Mankind won by
         TKO.

KING OF THE RING 1997–1998

1. b. Faarooq
2. d. Both men were disqualified.
3. c. Sycho Sid
4. b. Mankind
5. c. Pittsburgh
6. d. Ken Shamrock
7. c. Jerry Lawler
8. b. Bob Holly
9. c. Kane
10. c. Taka Michinoku

KING OF THE RING 1999–2000

1. b. Mr. Ass
2. d. Val Venis
3. b. They won Austin's 50 percent share in WWE.
4. c. Undertaker pinned The Rock.
5. b. Matt pinned Christian.

6. c. The Rock
7. c. Handicap
   Tables
   Dumpster
8. a. Val Venis
9. c. Edge & Christian
10. a. Evening Gown

KING OF THE RING 2001–2002

1. c. Raven
2. c. Rikishi
3. a. Booker T
4. b. X-Pac
5. b. Bubba Ray pinned Spike.
6. c. The Rock
7. b. Angle made Hogan submit.
8. d. Rob Van Dam
9. c. Jamie Noble
10. a. Molly Holly

SECTION XIV. *NO MERCY*

NO MERCY 1999–2000

1. b. Good Housekeeping
2. b. X-Pac
3. d. Fabulous Moolah
4. b. Ladder

5. b. The Rock
6. b. Goodfather & Bull Buchanan
7. d. No Disqualification
8. c. X-Pac

9. c. The match was declared no contest.
10. c. Billy Gunn

NO MERCY 2001–2002

1. d. Rob Van Dam
2. c. Christian
3. b. Big Show & Tajiri
4. c. Lingerie
5. b. Chris Jericho
6. b. Dawn Marie
7. a. Trish Stratus
8. d. Paul Heyman
9. c. Jamie Noble
10. a. Hurricane

NO MERCY 2003–2004

1. c. Linda McMahon
2. a. Matt Hardy
3. c. Shaniqua
4. d. Big Show
5. a. Bike Chain

6. c. John Cena
7. c. Rico pinned D-Von.
8. c. Kenzo Suzuki & Rene Dupree
9. b. Last Ride
10. b. Spike Dudley

NO MERCY 2005–2007

1. a. Eddie Guerrero
2. b. Christy Hemme pinned Melina.
3. b. Juventud
4. c. Sylvan
5. d. Randy & Bob Orton put Undertaker in the casket.
6. c. Finlay
7. b. Falls Count Anywhere
8. a. Ashley
9. b. Randy Orton
10. b. Beth Phoenix

SECTION XV. *TABOO TUESDAY/CYBER SUNDAY*

TABOO TUESDAY 2004–2005

1. b. Shelton Benjamin
2. d. Steel Cage
3. c. chain
4. a. Shawn Michaels

5. d. Milwaukee
6. b. Molly Holly
7. a. Cade & Murdoch
8. d. Vader & Goldust

9. c. lingerie

10. a. Triple H

CYBER SUNDAY 2006–2007

1. b. Eric Bischoff

2. a. Lita

3. c. King Booker

4. b. Cryme Tyme

5. c. Carlito

6. a. Mickie James

7. b. Miz

8. b. Kane

9. d. Street Fight

10. b. Steve Austin

SECTION XVI. SURVIVOR SERIES

SURVIVOR SERIES 1987–1989

1. b. Andre the Giant

2. d. Jumping Bomb
       Angels

3. d. Brutus Beefcake

4. d. Richfield

5. a. Thursday

6. b. Powers of Pain

7. d. Haku

8. d. Brutus Beefcake

9. d. Mr. Perfect

10. d. Greg Valentine

SURVIVOR SERIES 1990–1991

1. d. Tito Santana

2. c. Jim Duggan

3. c. Hercules

4. c. Ted DiBiase

5. a. Visionaries

6. c. Ric Flair

7. b. Beau Beverly

8. b. Ric Flair

9. b. I.R.S.

10. c. Gravest Challenge

SURVIVOR SERIES 1992–1993

1. a. Nasty Boys

2. b. Hart made Michaels
       submit.

3. c. Mr. Perfect

4. b. Yokozuna

5. a. Nightstick on
       a Pole

6. b. Owen Hart

7. b. White Knight

8. b. Lex Luger

9. c. Smokey Mountain
       Wrestling

10. b. Bushwackers & Men
        on a Mission

SURVIVOR SERIES 1994-1996

1. b.   Chuck Norris
2. d.   Razor Ramon
3. b.   Davey Boy Smith
4. b.   Guts 'n' Glory
5. d.   Bret Hart
6. a.   1-2-3 Kid
7. d.   Sycho Sid
8. a.   Sycho Sid
9. d.   No one survived
10. b. Mankind

SURVIVOR SERIES 1997-1998

1. b.   Davey Boy Smith
2. a.   Steve Austin
3. a.   Interrogator
4. c.   Goldust
5. d.   Ken Shamrock
6. c.   Montreal
7. b.   Kane
8. c.   Jeff Jarrett
9. b.   Sable
10. b. D'Lo Brown & Mark Henry

SURVIVOR SERIES 1999

1. c.   Al Snow
2. a.   Fabulous Moolah
3. b.   Steven Richard

4. c.   Chyna
5. c.   Shawn Stasiak
6. b.   British Bulldog
7. c.   Godfather & D'Lo Brown
8. a.   Hardcore Holly
9. c.   Big Show
10. c. Big Boss Man

SURVIVOR SERIES 2000-2001

1. c.   Eric
2. c.   Molly pinned Trish.
3. b.   K-Kwik
4. c.   No Disqualification
5. b.   Jeff Hardy
6. b.   Rob Van Dam
7. c.   Big Show
8. c.   Test
9. c.   Torrie Wilson
10. d. Steel Cage

SURVIVOR SERIES 2002-2003

1. b.   Hardcore
2. b.   Los Guerreros
3. a.   Bubba Ray Dudley
4. a.   o
5. c.   Billy Kidman
6. d.   Ambulance
7. d.   Randy Orton
8. a.   Kane

9. a. Molly Holly

10. c. Goldberg

SURVIVOR SERIES 2004–2005

1. c. Rob Van Dam
2. c. Spike Dudley
3. a. Randy Orton
4. b. Booker T
5. b. Shelton Benjamin
6. c. Last Man Standing
7. b. Randy Orton
8. c. Boogeyman
9. b. Daivari
10. d. Melina

SURVIVOR SERIES 2006–2007

1. c. Ric Flair
2. a. Lita
3. b. Bobby Lashley
4. c. First Blood
5. b. MVP
6. d. Shawn Michaels
7. b. Mickie James
8. c. MVP
9. a. Murdoch pinned Rhodes.
10. b. Finlay

SECTION XVII. *ARMAGEDDON*

ARMAGEDDON 1999

1. c. No Holds Barred
2. b. Big Boss Man
3. d. Miss Kitty
4. c. Acolytes
5. c. Miss Kitty
6. c. Al Snow
7. b. Val Venis
8. d. X-Pac
9. c. Rikishi
10. b. Fabulous Moolah and Mae Young

ARMAGEDDON 2000–2002

1. c. Dean Malenko
2. d. Edge & Christian
3. c. The Rock
4. a. Last Man Standing
5. c. Val Venis
6. c. steel cage
7. c. Booker T & Goldust
8. b. Kurt Angle
9. b. Victoria
10. d. A-Train was disqualified.

ARMAGEDDON 2003–2004

1. b. Theodore Long
2. b. Batista &
        Ric Flair
3. c. Mick Foley
4. a. Goldberg
5. a. Christian
6. b. Booker T
7. a. Big Show
8. c. Funaki
9. b. Jesus
10. a. Kurt Angle

ARMAGEDDON 2005–2006

1. d. Kid Kash
2. a. Joey Mercury
3. b. Big Show & Kane
4. a. JBL
5. c. Paul Birchill
6. c. Last Ride
7. a. Batista
8. a. Paul London & Brian
        Kendrick
9. b. Inferno
10. c. Jimmy Wang Yang

ACKNOWLEDGMENTS

I'd like to thank my wife, Fran; my three children, John, Alice, and Margaret; and my parents, Mary and Norman, for their support in everything I do.

Thanks to everyone at WWE who makes it such a comfortable and enjoyable place to work, and Margaret Clark and everyone at Simon & Schuster for helping me turn a jumble of questions and answers into the book you are holding.